EASY PIANO

CASTING CROWNS
THE ALTAR AND THE DOOR

ISBN-13: 978-1-4234-5285-0
ISBN-10: 1-4234-5285-2

HAL•LEONARD®
CORPORATION

7777 W. BLUEMOUND RD. P.O. BOX 13819 MILWAUKEE, WI 53213

Visit Hal Leonard Online at
www.halleonard.com

WHAT THIS WORLD NEEDS

Words and Music by MARK HALL
and HECTOR CERVANTES

With a driving beat

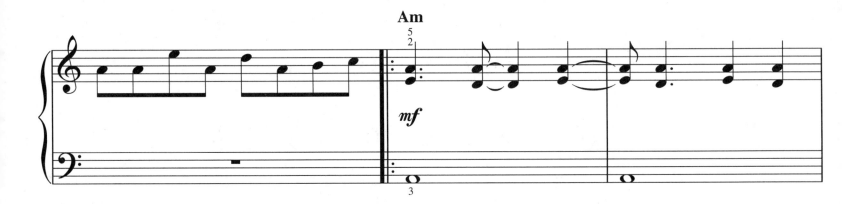

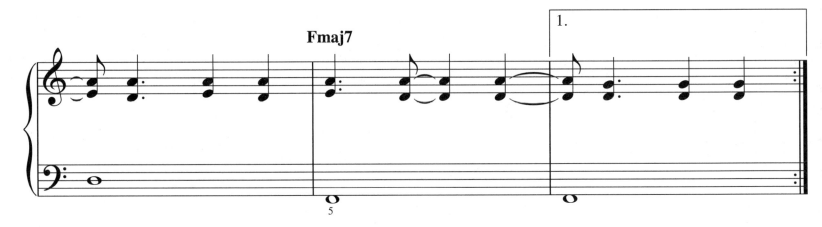

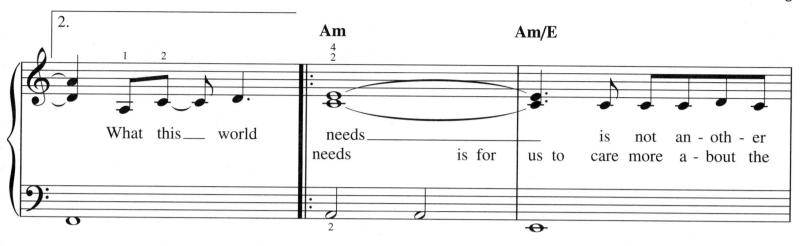

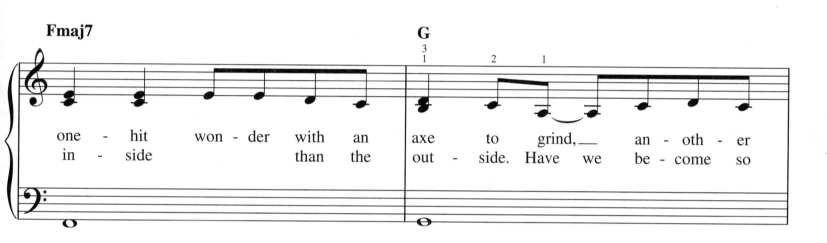

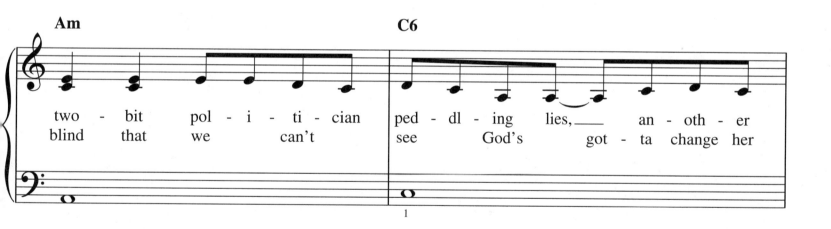

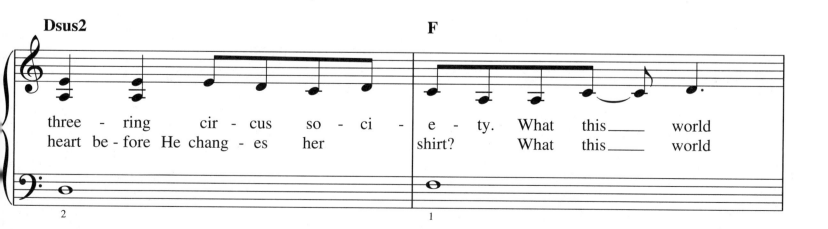

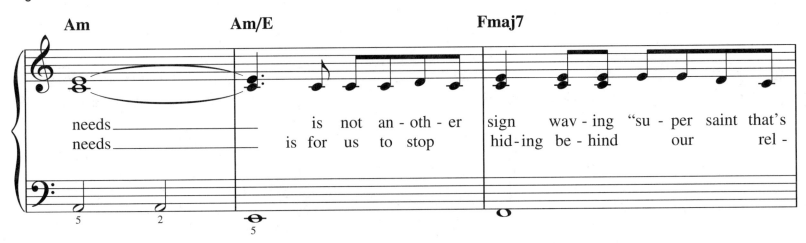

needs_____ is not an - oth - er sign wav - ing "su - per saint that's
needs_____ is for us to stop hid-ing be - hind our rel -

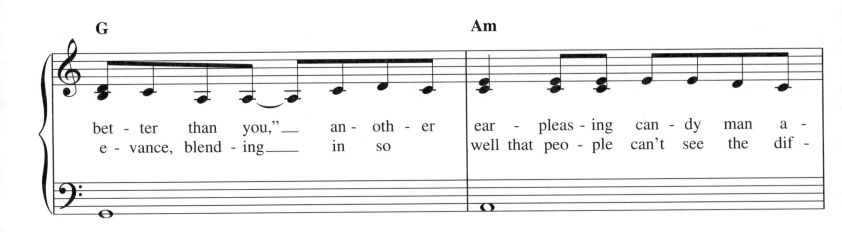

bet - ter than you,"__ an - oth - er ear - pleas - ing can - dy man a -
e - vance, blend - ing___ in so well that peo - ple can't see the dif -

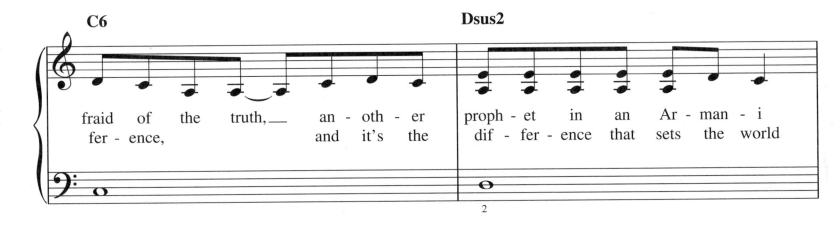

fraid of the truth,__ an - oth - er proph - et in an Ar - man - i
fer - ence, and it's the dif - fer - ence that sets the world

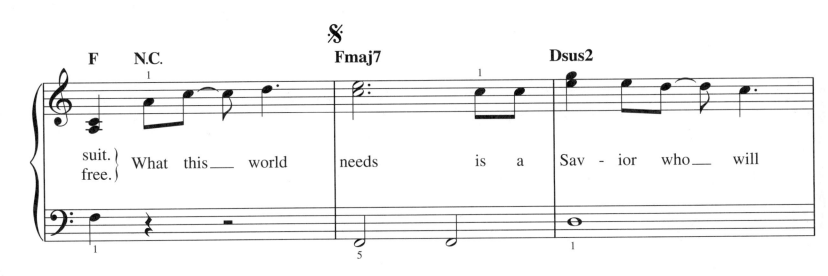

suit.
free. } What this__ world needs is a Sav - ior who__ will

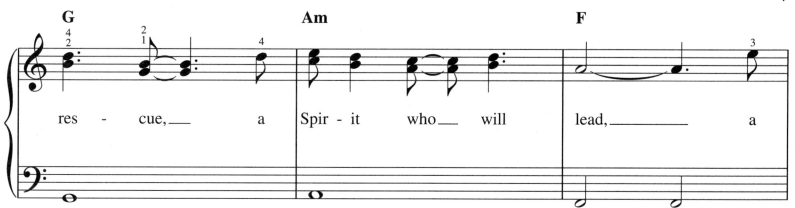

res - cue,_____ a Spir - it who___ will lead,_____ a

Fa - ther who___ will love them___ in their time___ of

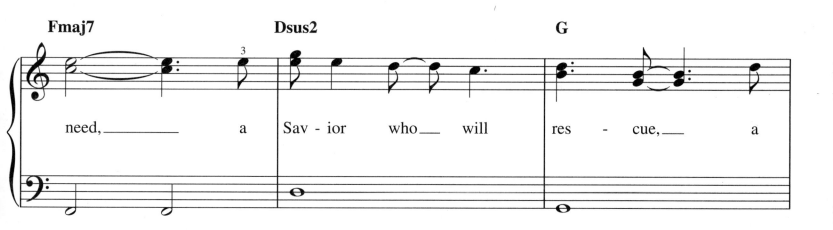

need,_____ a Sav - ior who___ will res - cue,___ a

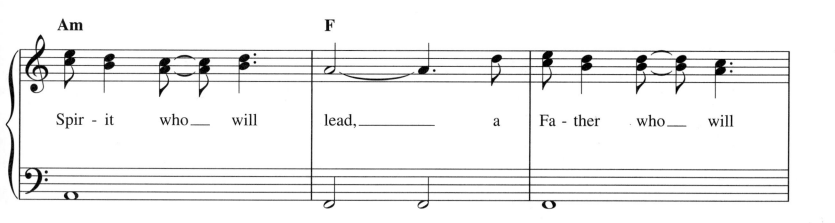

Spir - it who___ will lead,_____ a Fa - ther who___ will

G **To Coda** ⊕ **1.** **Am**

love. That's what this ___ world needs.

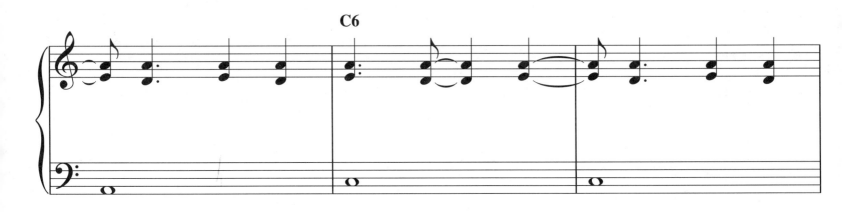

C6

Dsus2 **Fmaj7**

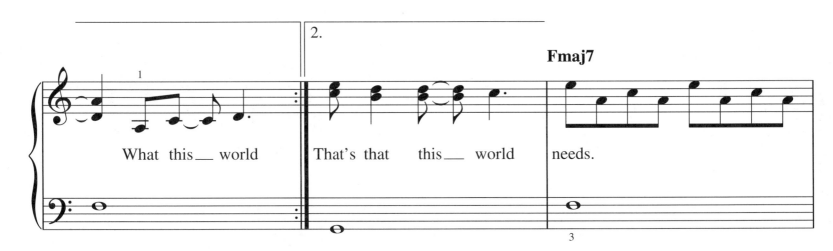

2. **Fmaj7**

What this ___ world That's that this ___ world needs.

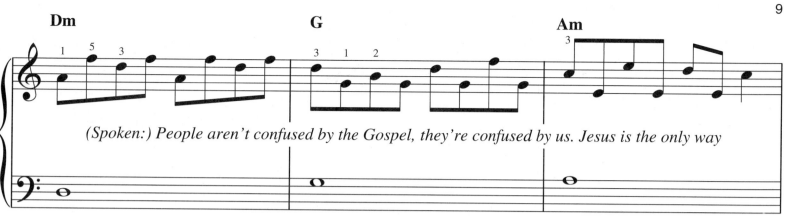

(Spoken:) People aren't confused by the Gospel, they're confused by us. Jesus is the only way

to God, but we are not the only way to Jesus. This world doesn't need my tie, my hoodie,

my denomination or my translation of the Bible. They just need Jesus. We can be passionate

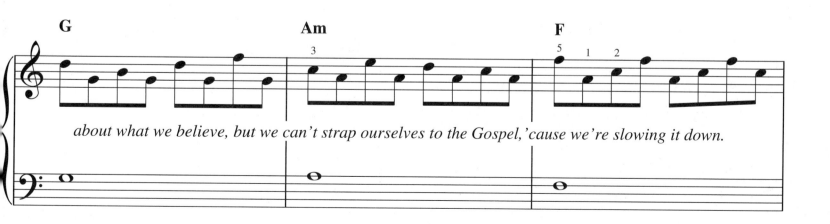

about what we believe, but we can't strap ourselves to the Gospel, 'cause we're slowing it down.

Jesus is going to save the world, but maybe the best thing we can do is just get out of the way.

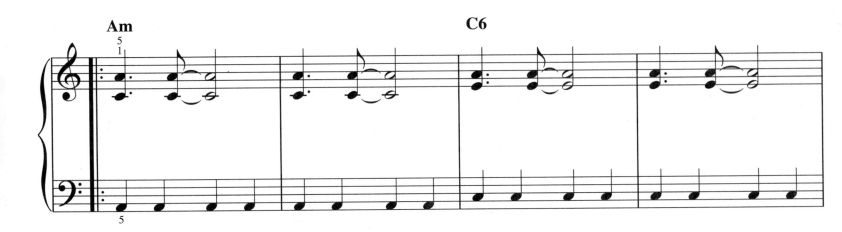

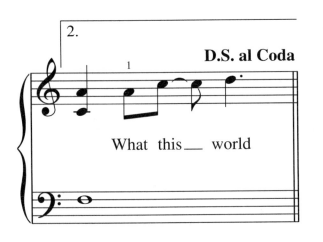

What this _ world

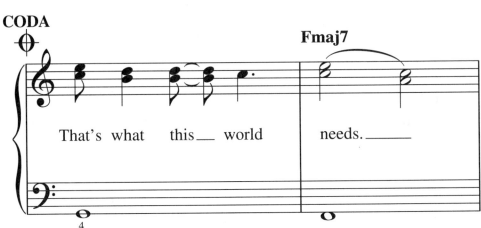

That's what this _ world needs. _

Je -sus is—— our   Sav - ior,——   that's what this—— world   needs.—— A

Fa -ther's arms—— a - round you,   that's what this—— world   needs.——

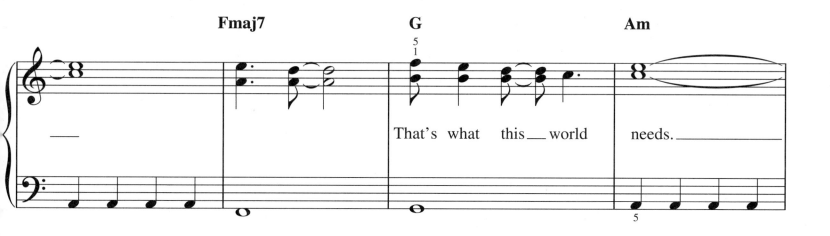

——   That's what this—— world   needs.——

——

EVERY MAN

Words and Music by MARK HALL,
NICHOLE NORDEMAN and BERNIE HERMS

I'm the man with all___ I've ev - er want - ed, all the toys___ and play - ing

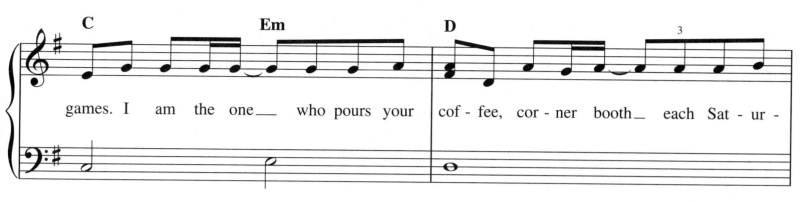

games. I am the one __ who pours your cof - fee, cor - ner booth __ each Sat - ur -

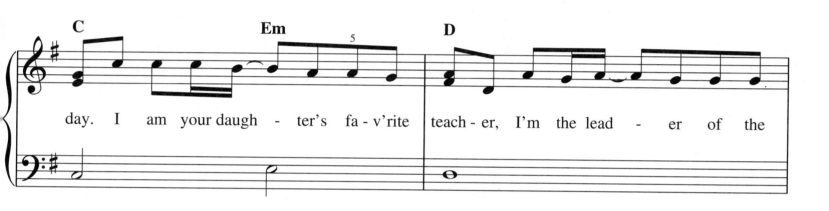

day. I am your daugh - ter's fa - v'rite teach - er, I'm the lead - er of the

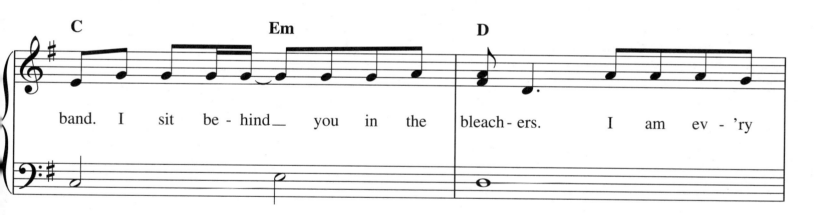

band. I sit be - hind __ you in the bleach - ers. I am ev - 'ry

man. I'm the coach of ev - 'ry win - ning team, and still a los - er in my

mind. I am the sol - dier in the air - port fac - ing gi - ants one more

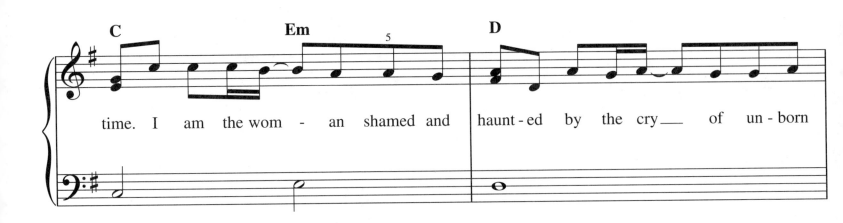

time. I am the wom - an shamed and haunt - ed by the cry___ of un - born

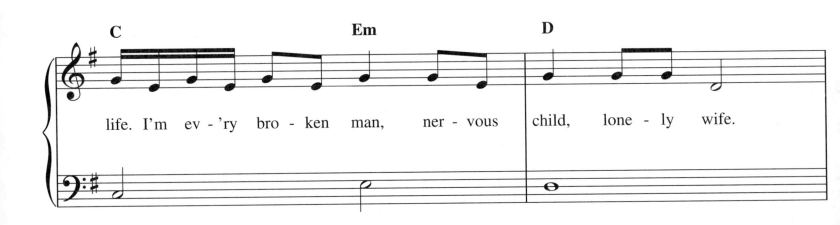

life. I'm ev - 'ry bro - ken man, ner - vous child, lone - ly wife.

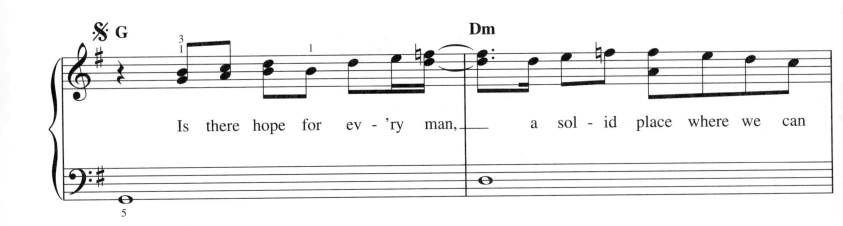

Is there hope for ev - 'ry man,___ a sol - id place where we can

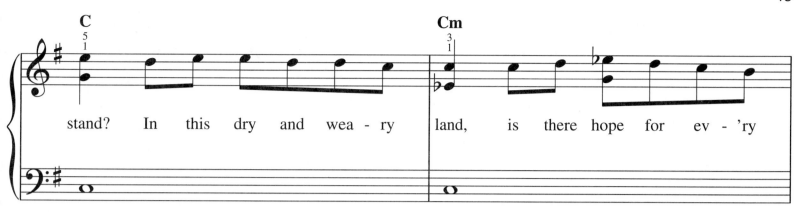

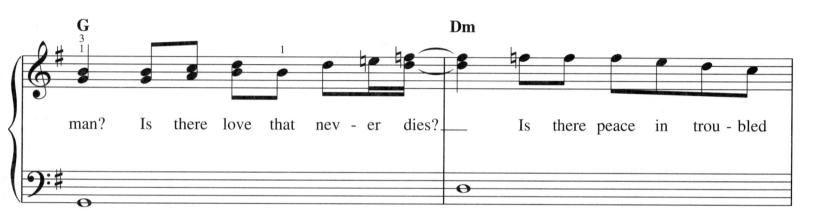

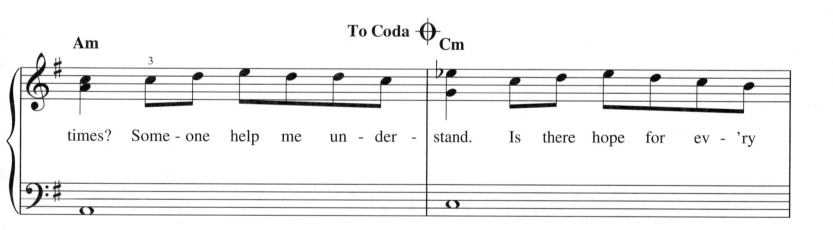

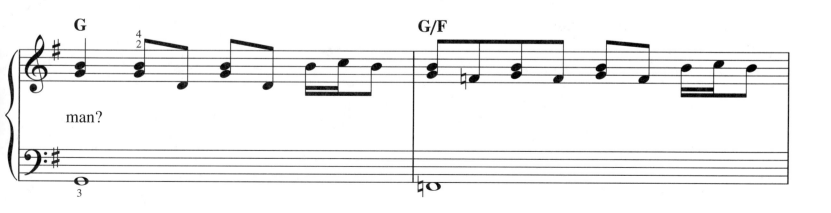

It seems there's just so man-y roads to trav- el; it's hard to tell where they will

lead. My life is scarred and my dreams un - rav - eled, and now I'm scared to take the

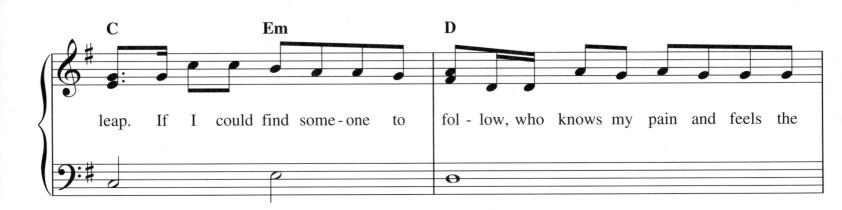

leap. If I could find some-one to fol - low, who knows my pain and feels the

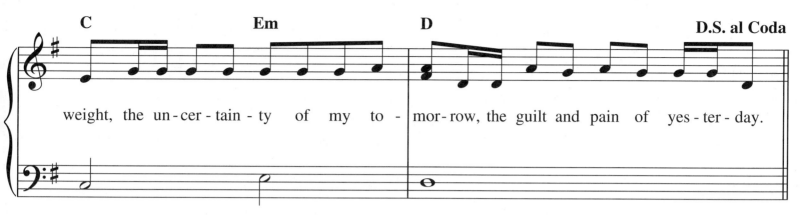

C **Em** **D** **D.S. al Coda**

weight, the un - cer - tain - ty of my to - mor - row, the guilt and pain of yes - ter - day.

CODA **Cm** **Em**

stand. Is there hope for ev - 'ry man?

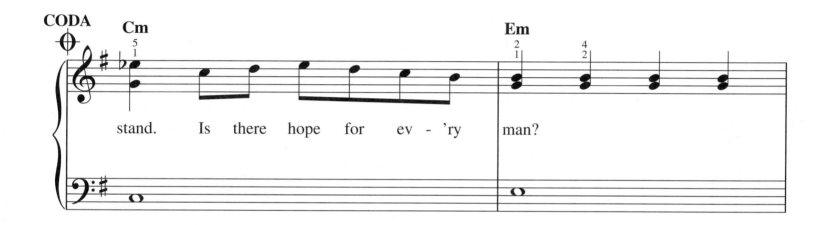

C **Gsus** **G** **D**

Am **C6** **Em**

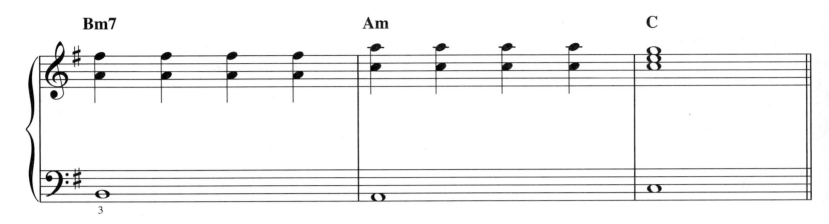

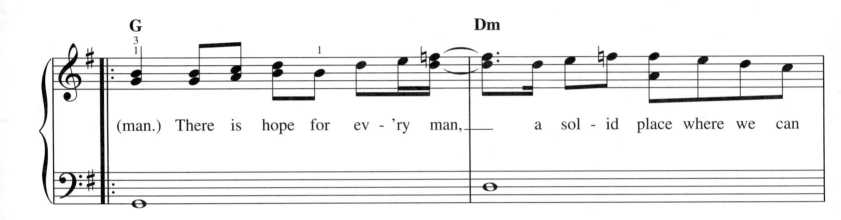

(man.) There is hope for ev - 'ry man,___ a sol - id place where we can

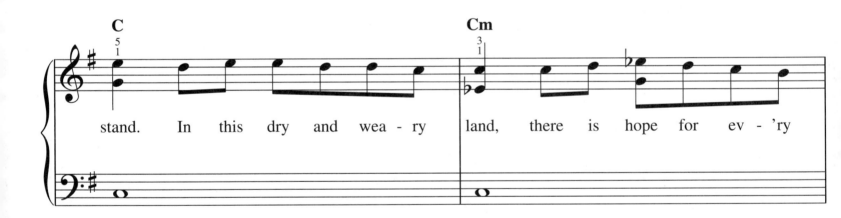

stand. In this dry and wea - ry land, there is hope for ev - 'ry

man. There is love that nev - er dies,___ there is peace in trou - bled

times. Will we help them un - der - stand? Je - sus is hope for ev - 'ry

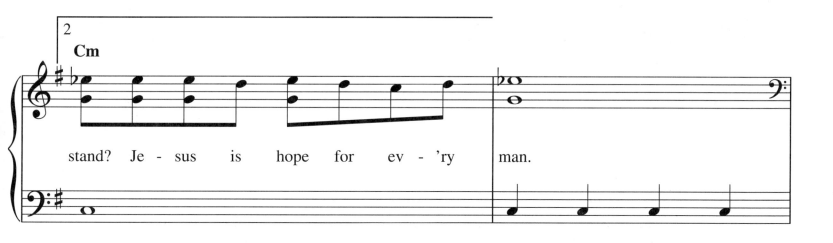

stand? Je - sus is hope for ev - 'ry man.

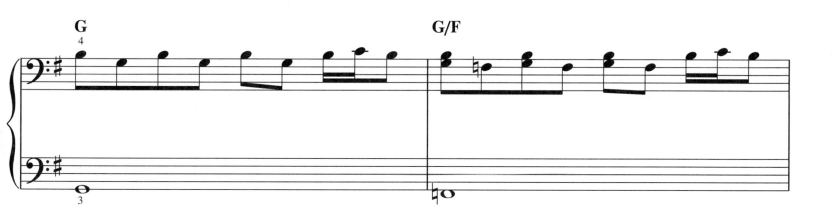

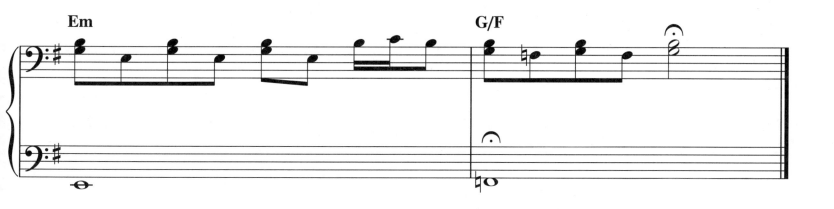

SLOW FADE

Words and Music by
MARK HALL

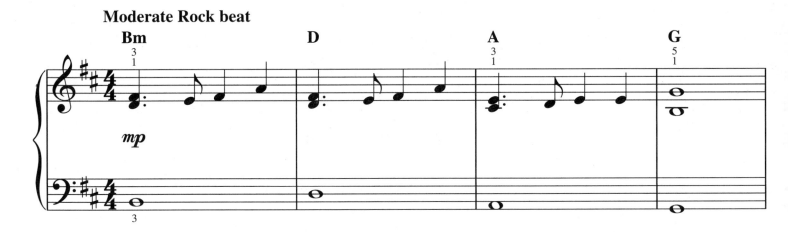

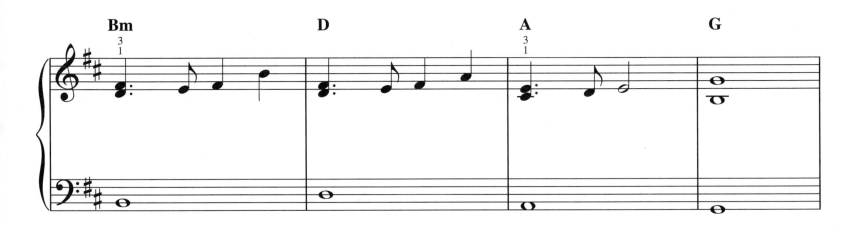

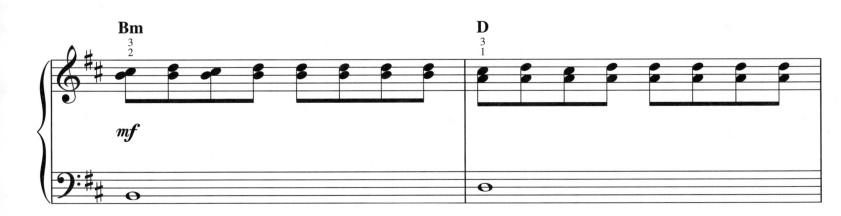

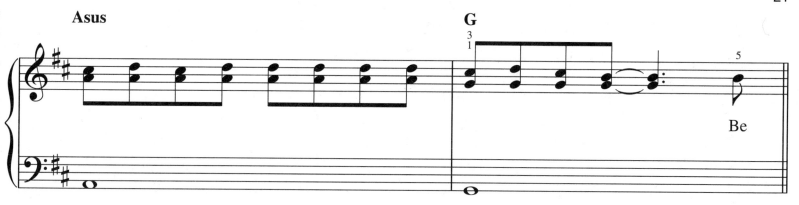

Asus ... **G**

Be

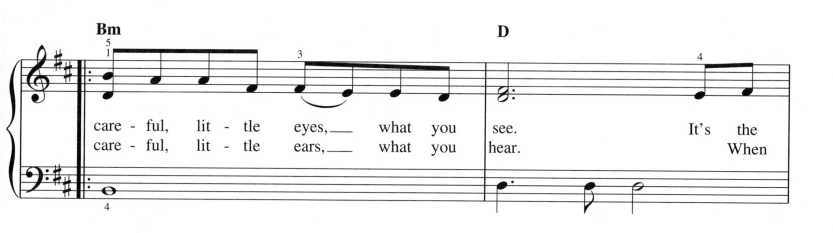

Bm ... **D**

care - ful, lit - tle eyes,___ what you see. It's the
care - ful, lit - tle ears,___ what you hear. When

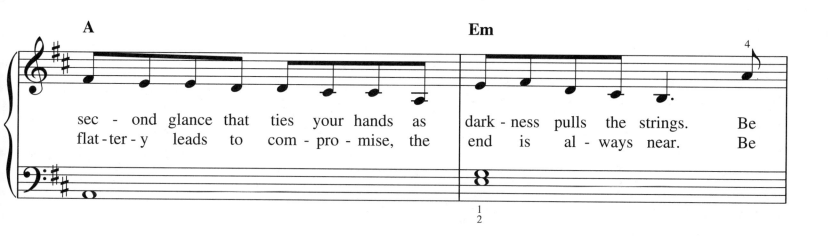

A ... **Em**

sec - ond glance that ties your hands as dark - ness pulls the strings. Be
flat - ter - y leads to com - pro - mise, the end is al - ways near. Be

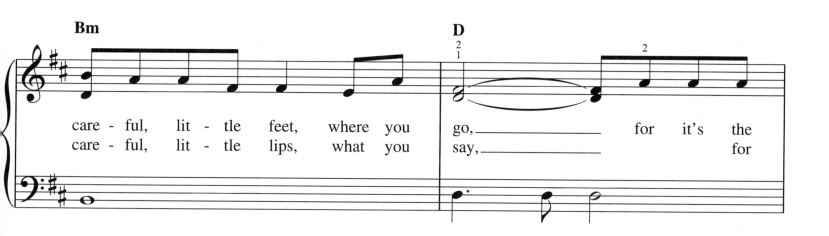

Bm ... **D**

care - ful, lit - tle feet, where you go,_____ for it's the
care - ful, lit - tle lips, what you say,_____ for

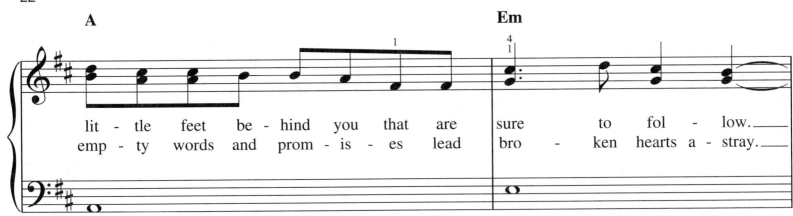

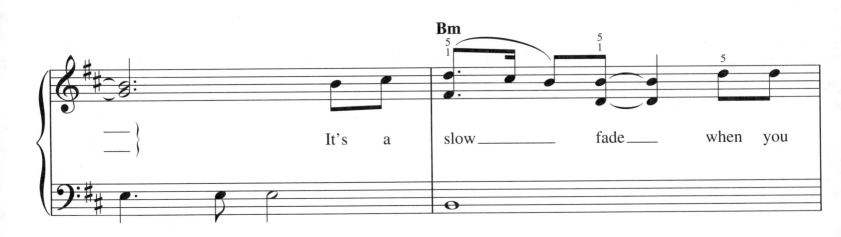

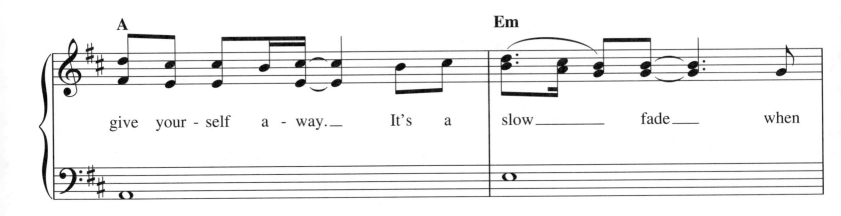

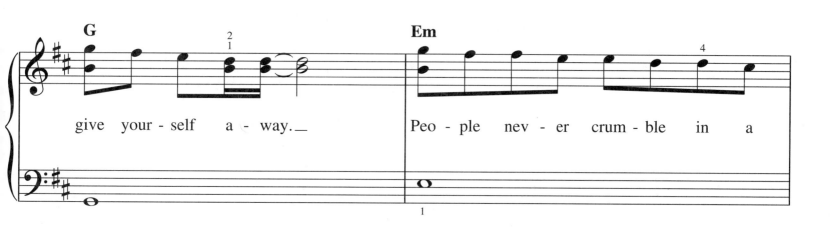

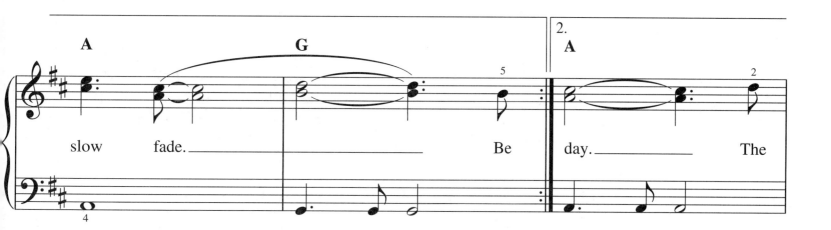

23

jour - ney from your mind to your hands is short - er than you're

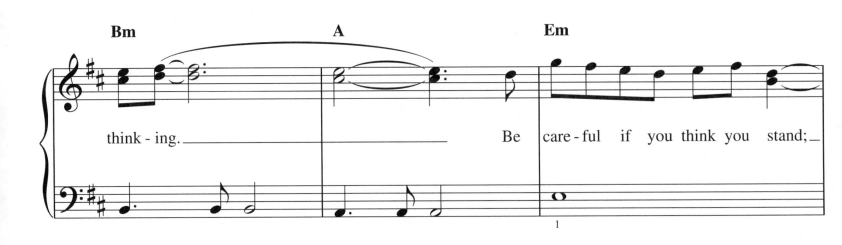

think - ing._____ Be care - ful if you think you stand;___

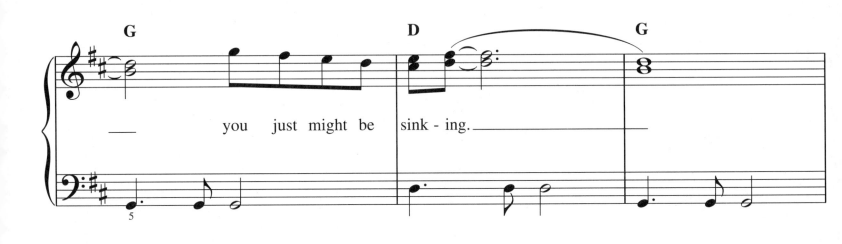

___ you just might be sink - ing._____

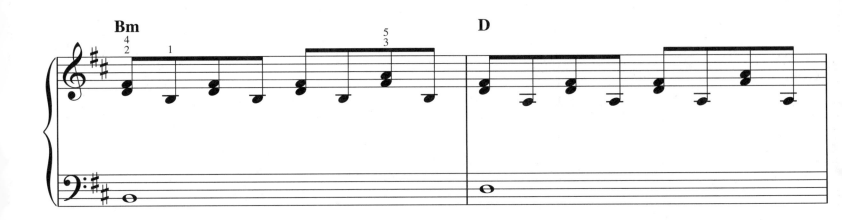

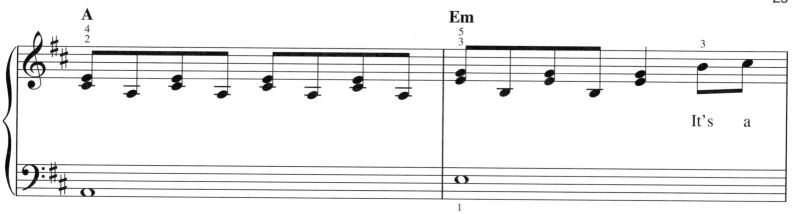

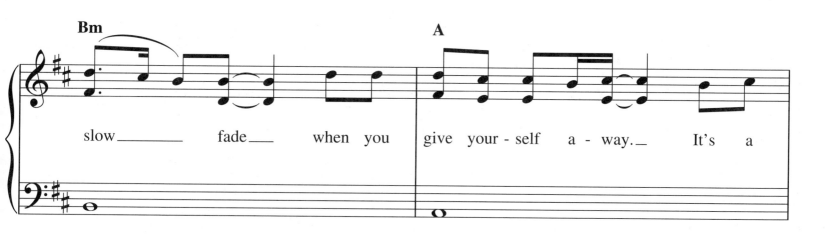

slow_____ fade___ when you give your-self a-way.___ It's a

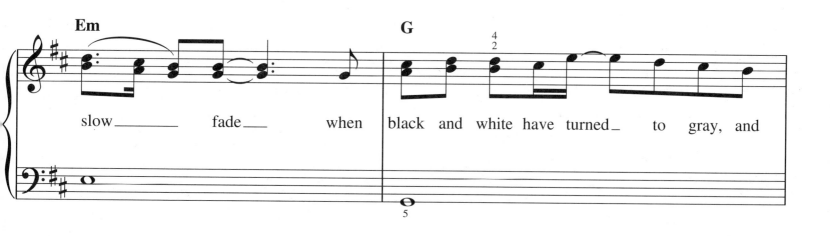

slow_____ fade___ when black and white have turned__ to gray, and

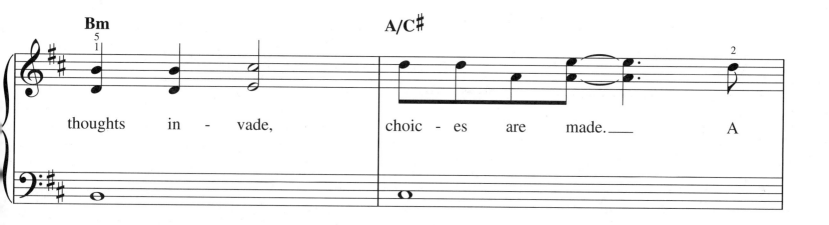

thoughts in-vade, choic-es are made.___ A

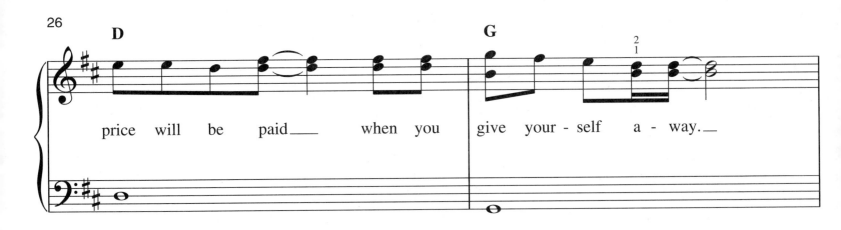

price will be paid___ when you give your - self a - way.___

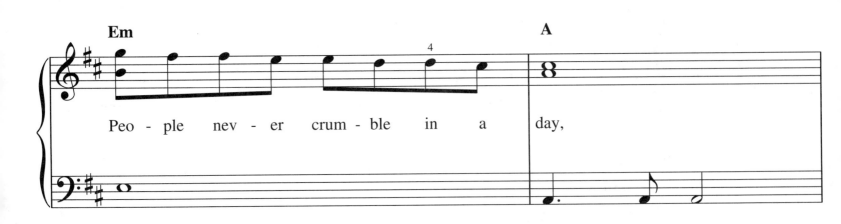

Peo - ple nev - er crum - ble in a day,

dad - dies nev - er crum - ble in a day,

fam - 'lies nev - er crum - ble in a day. *Child:* Oh, be

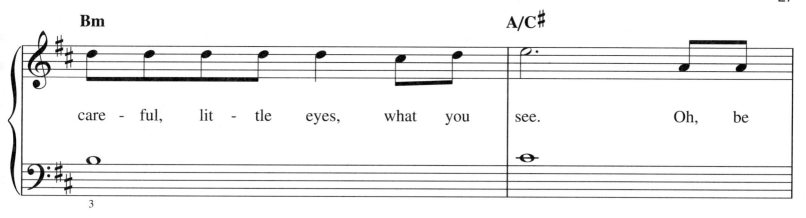

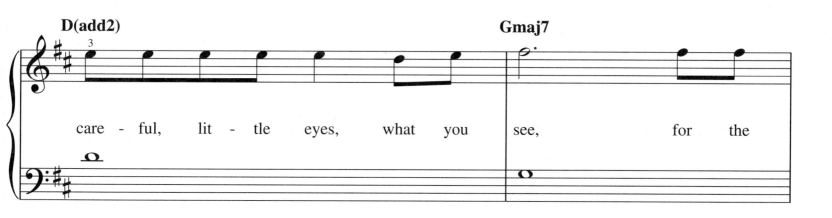

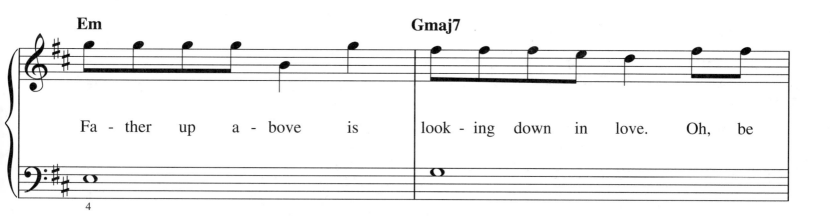

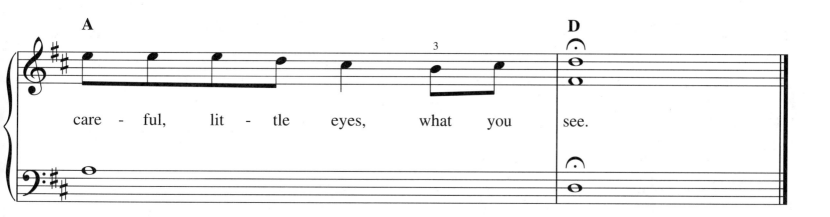

EAST TO WEST

Words and Music by MARK HALL
and BERNIE HERMS

Moderate Rock beat

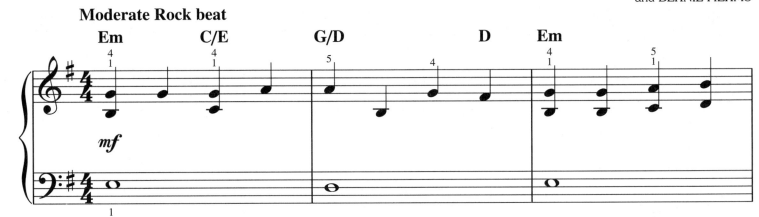

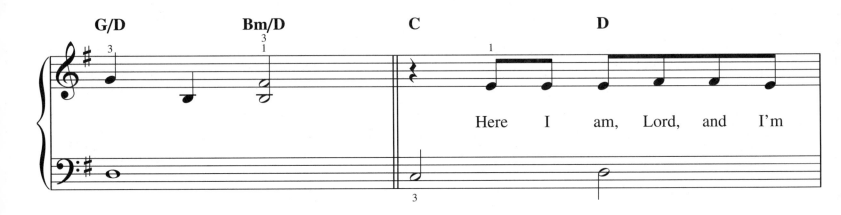

Here I am, Lord, and I'm

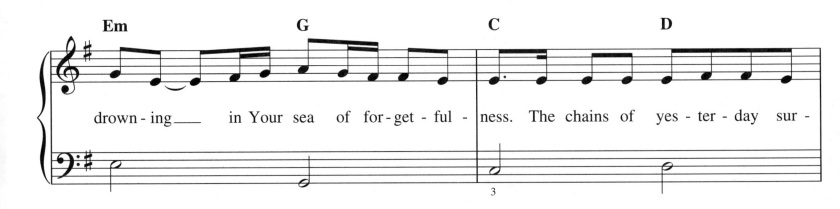

drown-ing ___ in Your sea of for-get-ful-ness. The chains of yes-ter-day sur-

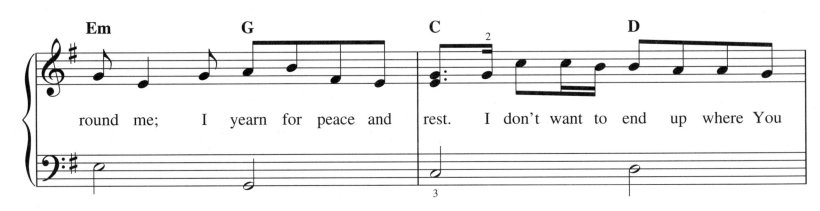

round me; I yearn for peace and rest. I don't want to end up where You

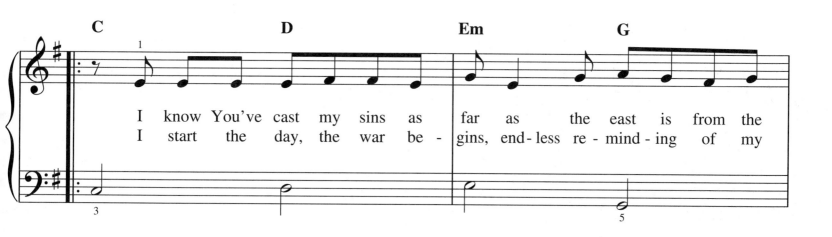

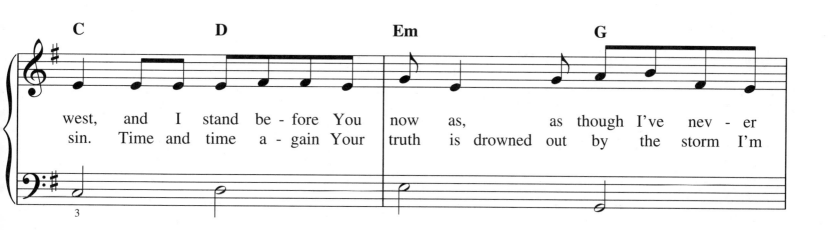

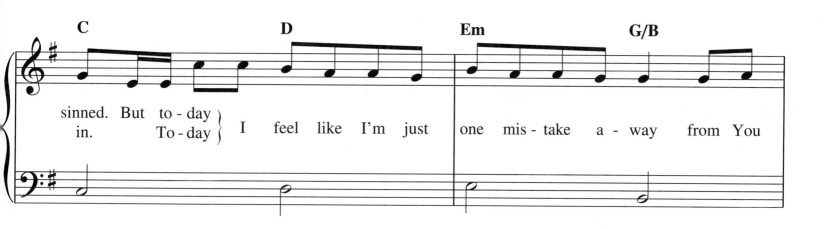

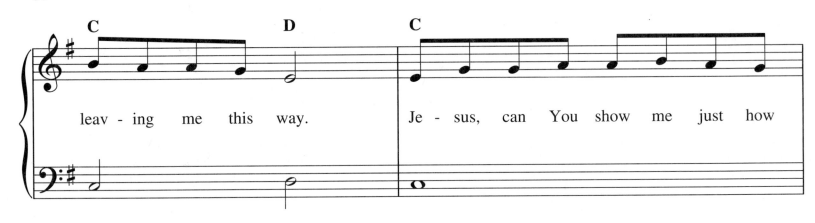

leav - ing me this way. Je - sus, can You show me just how

far the east is from the west? 'Cause I can't

bear to see the man I've been come ris - ing up in me a - gain. In the

arms of Your mer - cy I find rest, 'cause You know

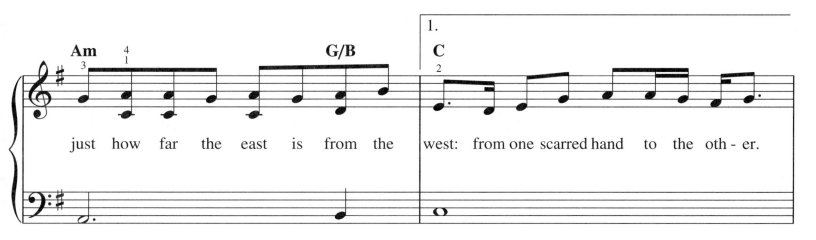

just how far the east is from the west: from one scarred hand to the oth - er.

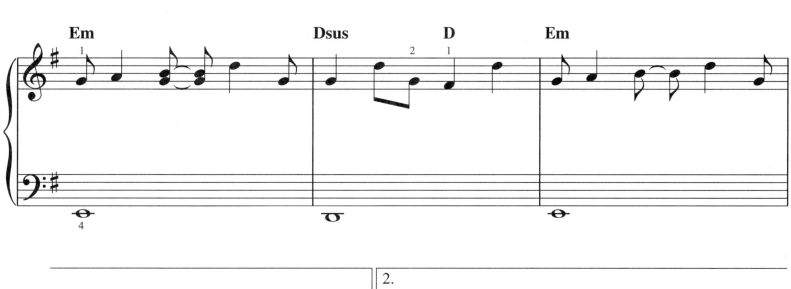

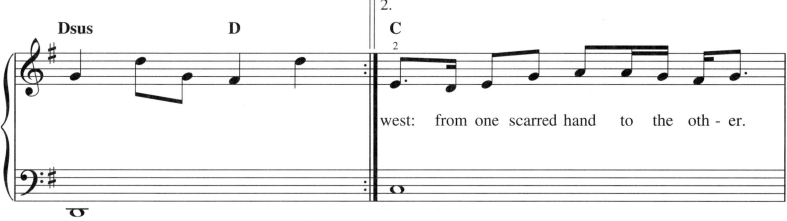

west: from one scarred hand to the oth - er.

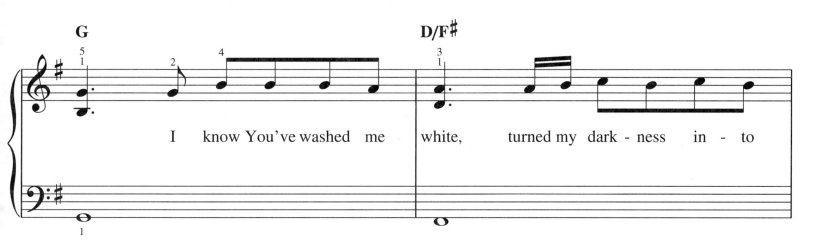

I know You've washed me white, turned my dark - ness in - to

light. I need Your peace to get me through, to get me through this

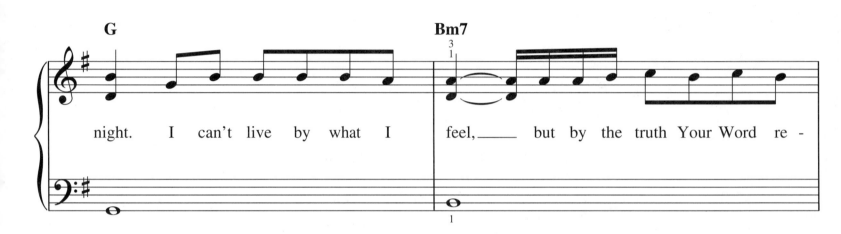

night. I can't live by what I feel,_____ but by the truth Your Word re-

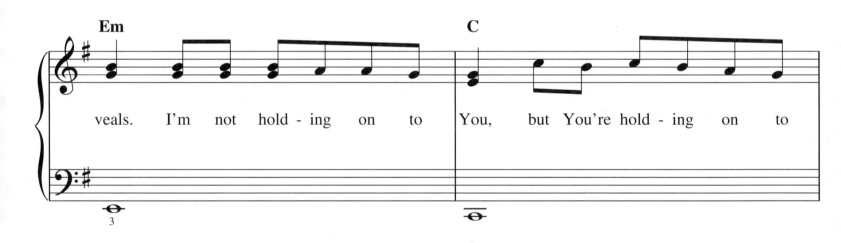

veals. I'm not hold - ing on to You, but You're hold - ing on to

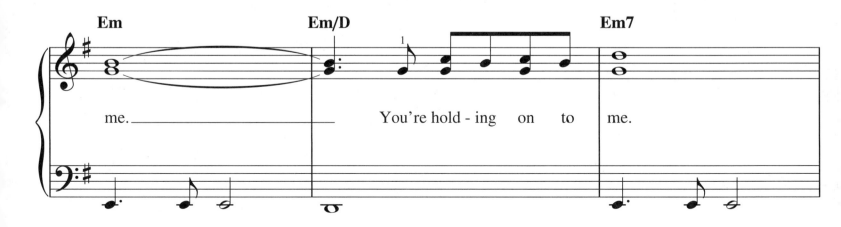

me._____ You're hold - ing on to me.

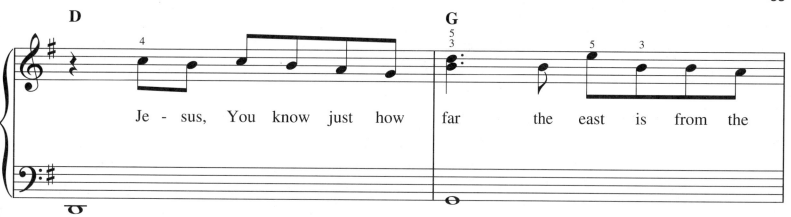

Je - sus, You know just how far the east is from the

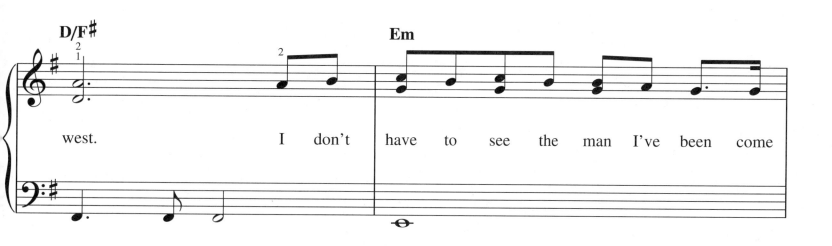

west. I don't have to see the man I've been come

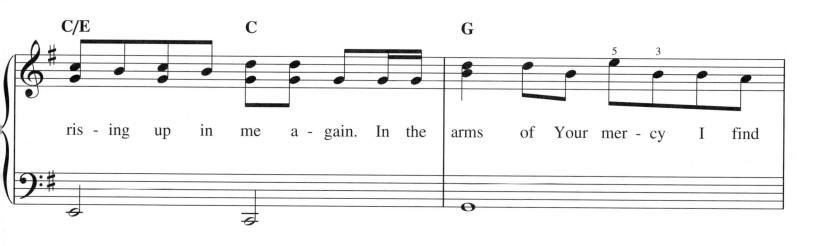

ris - ing up in me a - gain. In the arms of Your mer - cy I find

rest,_____ 'cause You know just how far the east is from the

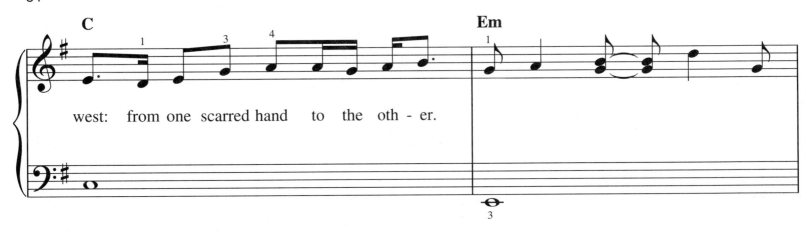

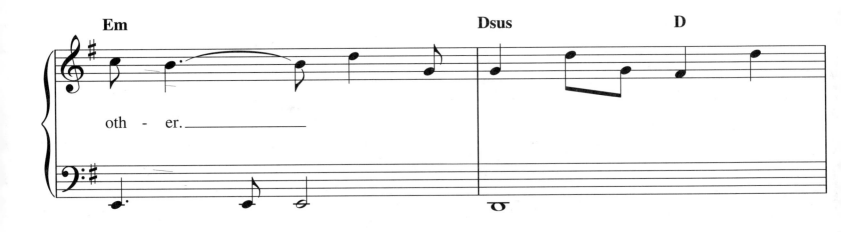

THE WORD IS ALIVE

Words and Music by MARK HALL
and STEVEN CURTIS CHAPMAN

36

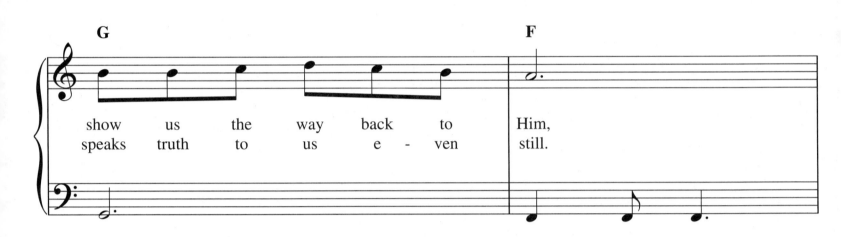

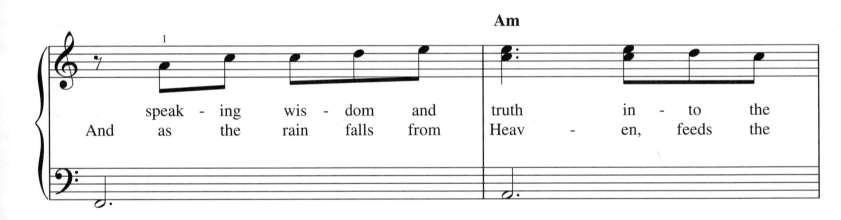

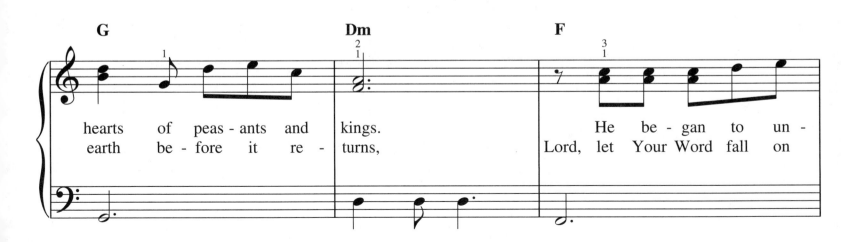

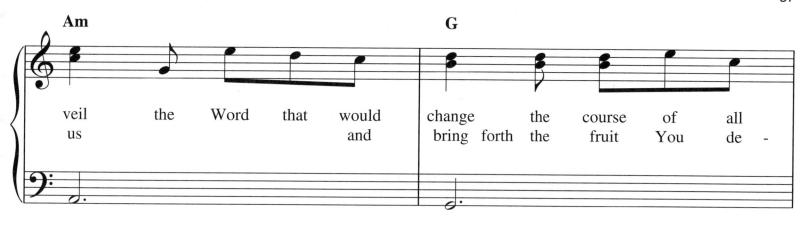

veil the Word that would
us and

change the course of all
bring forth the fruit You de -

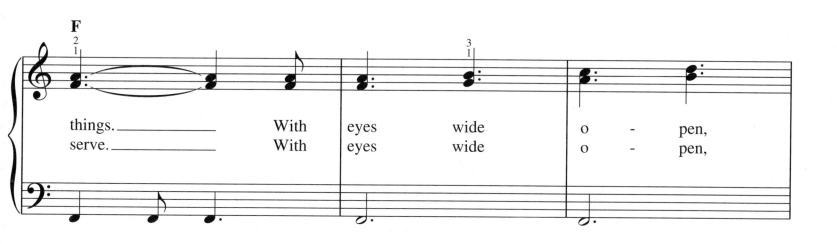

things._____ With eyes wide o - pen,
serve._____ With eyes wide o - pen,

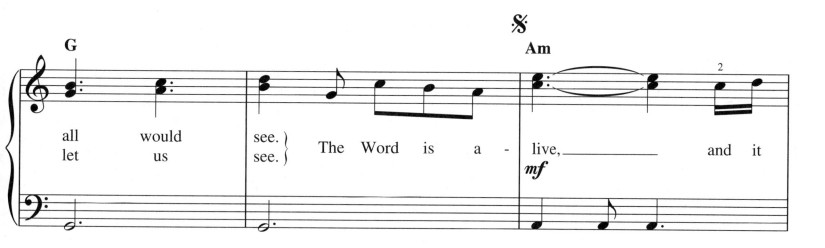

all would see.) The Word is a - live,_____ and it
let us see.)

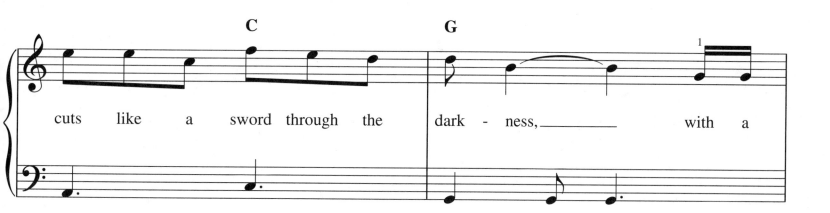

cuts like a sword through the dark - ness,_____ with a

mes - sage of life to the hope - less _____ and a - fraid, _____ breath - ing

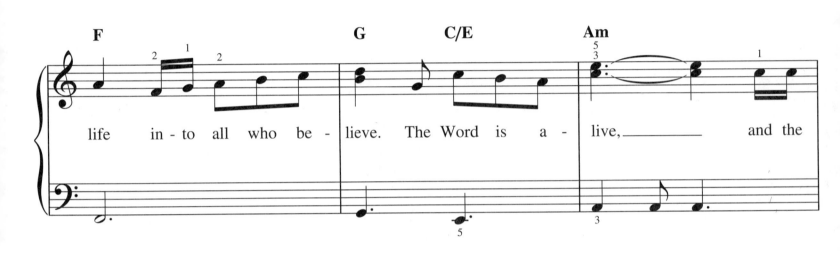

life in - to all who be - lieve. The Word is a - live, _____ and the

world and its glo - ries will fade, _____ but His truth, it will not pass a -

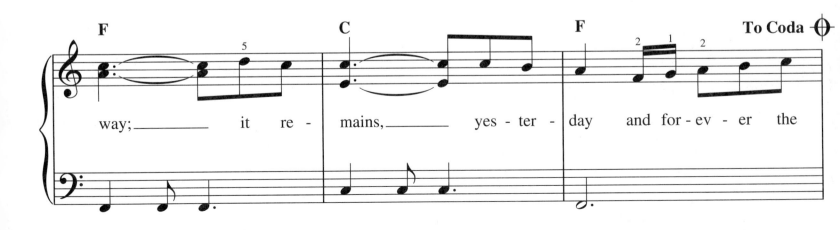

way; _____ it re - mains, _____ yes - ter - day and for - ev - er the

same. The Word is a - live.

same. The Word is a -

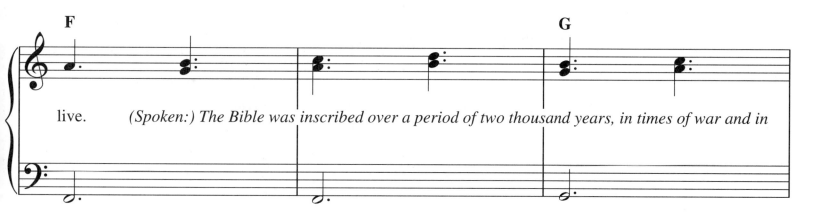

live. *(Spoken:) The Bible was inscribed over a period of two thousand years, in times of war and in*

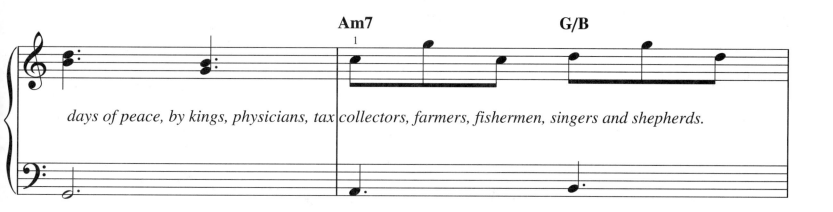

days of peace, by kings, physicians, tax collectors, farmers, fishermen, singers and shepherds.

C   **Dm7**   **G/B**   **C**

The marvel is that a library so perfectly cohesive could have been produced by such a diverse

Em7   **C/E**   **F**   **Dm7**

crowd over a period of time which staggers the imagination. Jesus is its grand subject, our good

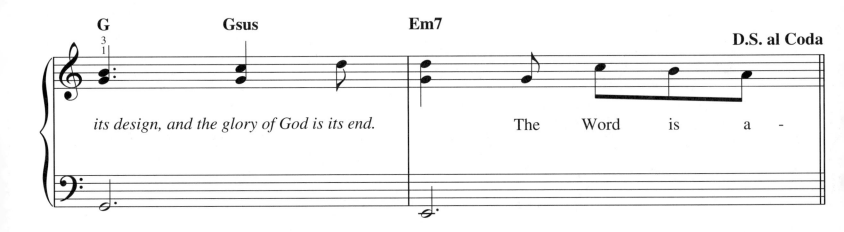

G   **Gsus**   **Em7**   **D.S. al Coda**

its design, and the glory of God is its end.   The   Word   is   a -

CODA   **G**   **Fmaj7**   **G6**

same.   The   Word   is   a - live.

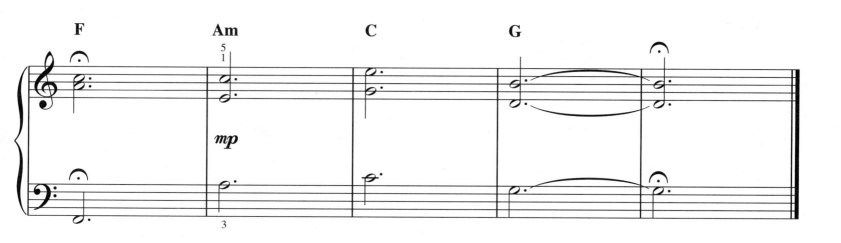

THE ALTAR AND THE DOOR

Words and Music by
MARK HALL

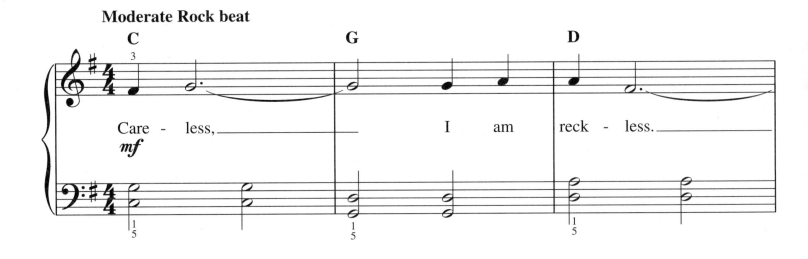

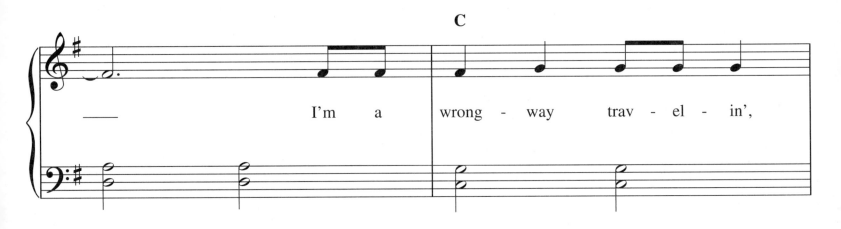

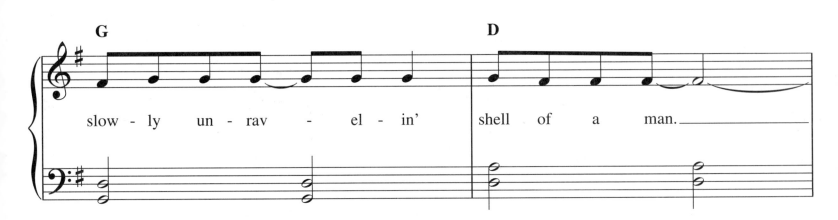

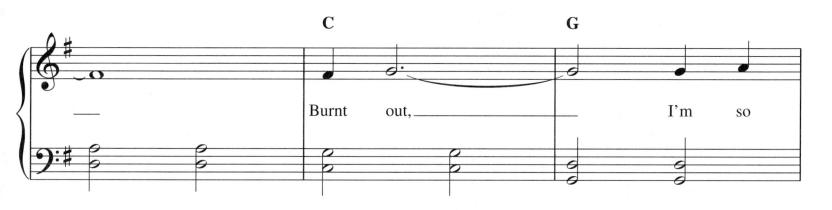

Burnt out, _____ I'm so

numb now _____ that the fire's just an em - ber way

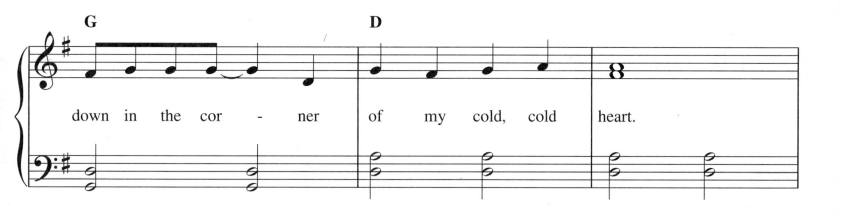

down in the cor - ner of my cold, cold heart.

Lord, this time I'll make it right. Here at the

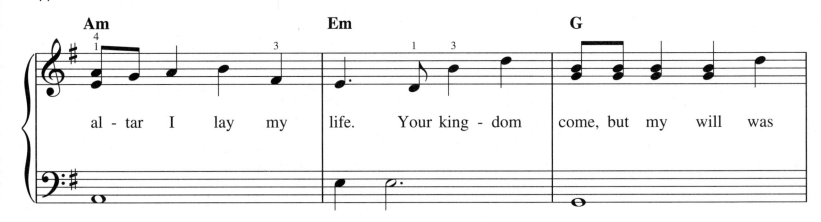

al - tar I lay my life. Your king - dom come, but my will was

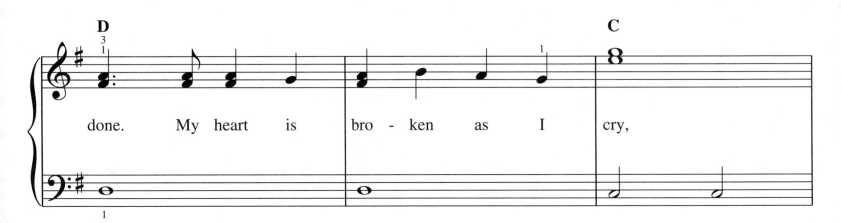

done. My heart is bro - ken as I cry,

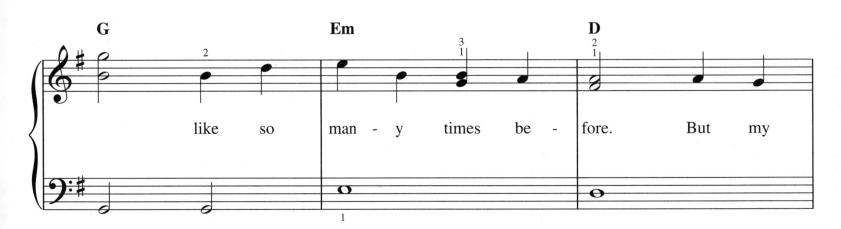

like so man - y times be - fore. But my

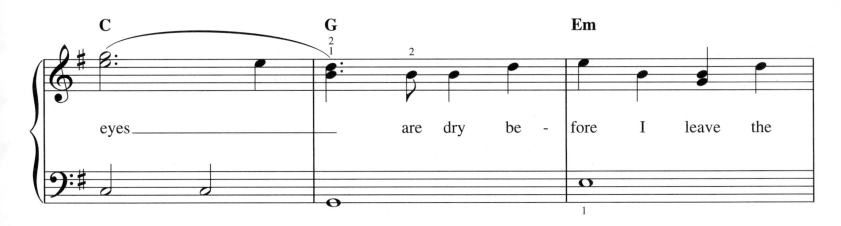

eyes_____ are dry be - fore I leave the

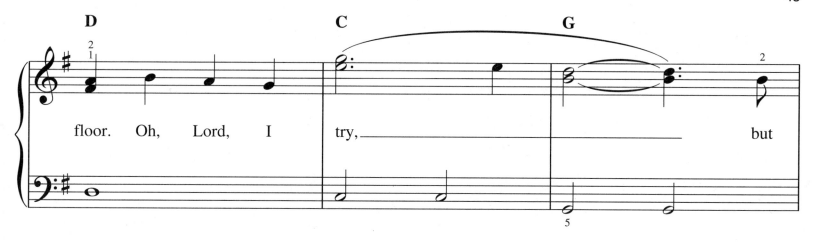

floor. Oh, Lord, I try, but

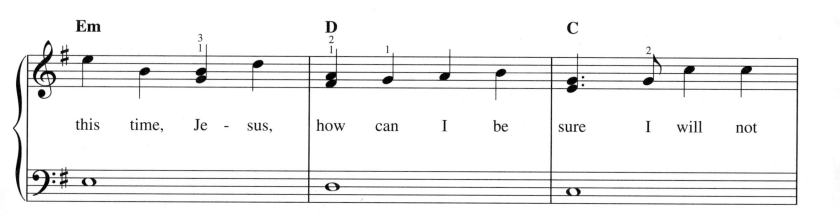

this time, Je - sus, how can I be sure I will not

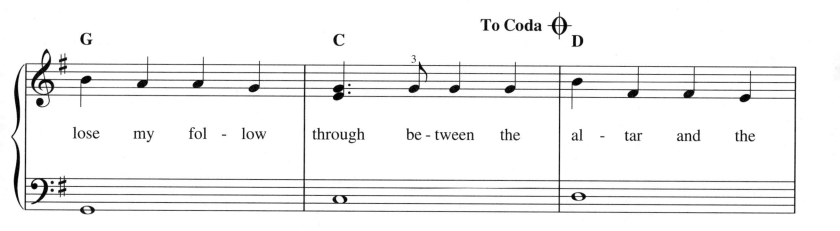

To Coda

lose my fol - low through be - tween the al - tar and the

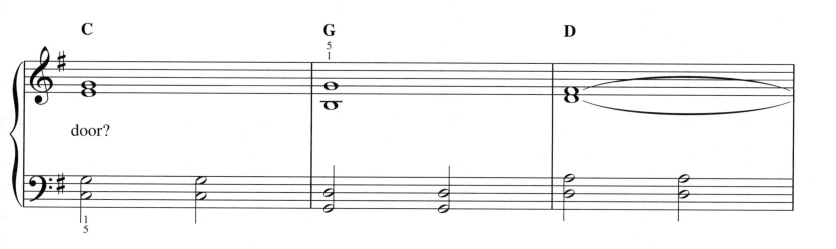

door?

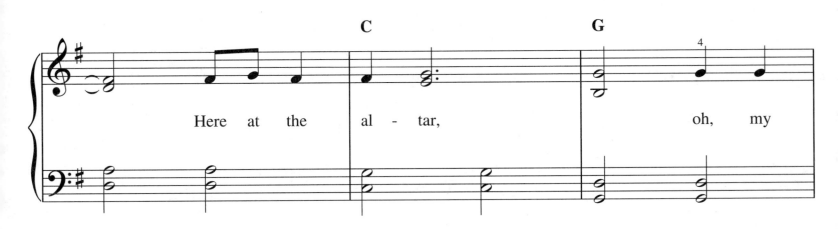

Here at the al - tar, oh, my

world's so black and white. How could I ev - er fal - ter

D.S. al Coda

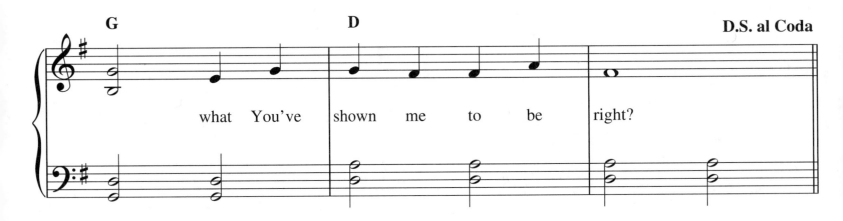

what You've shown me to be right?

CODA

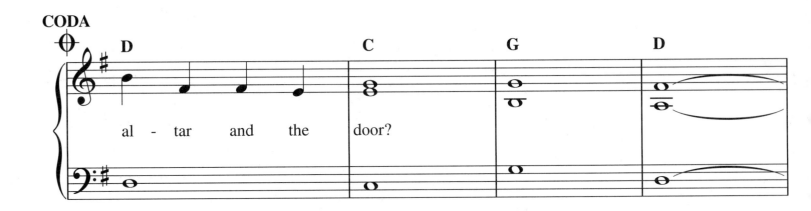

al - tar and the door?

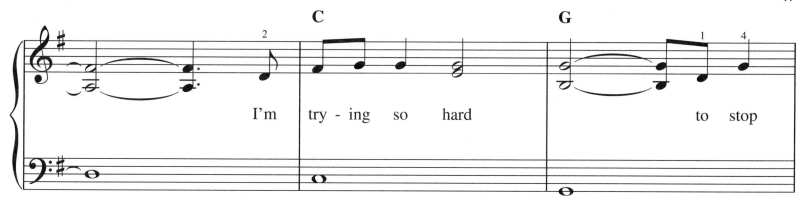

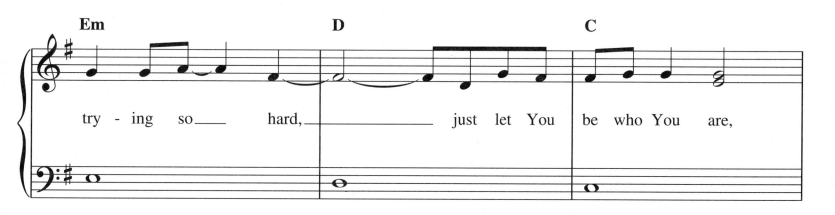

just let You be who You are, _____ Lord,

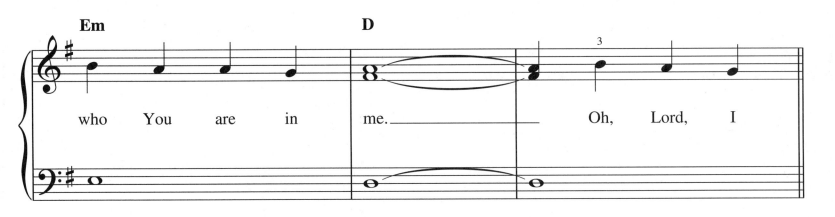

who You are in me. _____ Oh, Lord, I

cry,
(door?) like so man - y times be -

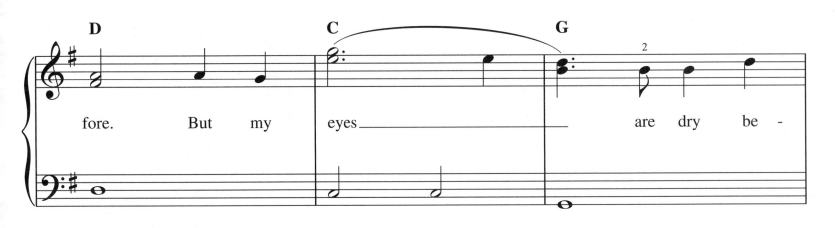

fore. But my eyes _____ are dry be -

fore I leave the floor. Oh, Lord, I try,_____

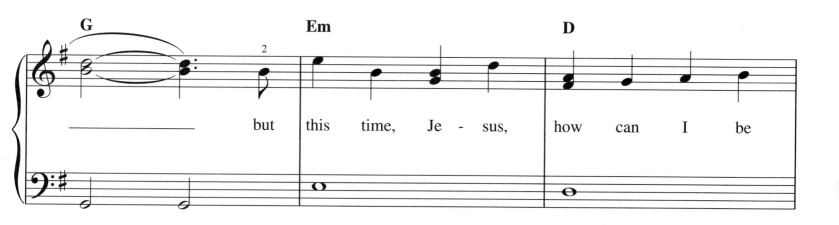

_____ but this time, Je - sus, how can I be

sure I will not lose my fol - low through be - tween the

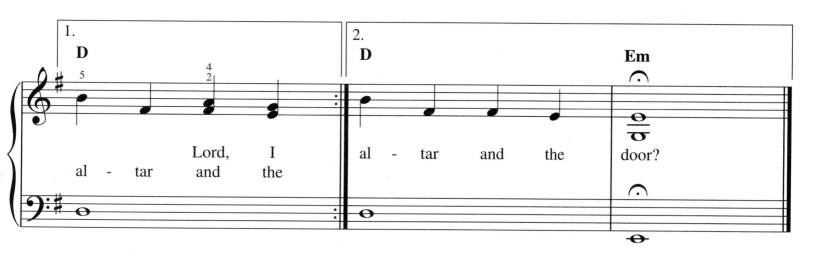

1.
Lord, I
al - tar and the

2.
al - tar and the door?

SOMEWHERE IN THE MIDDLE

Words and Music by
MARK HALL

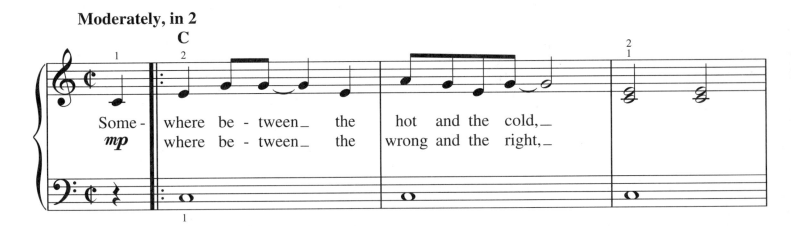

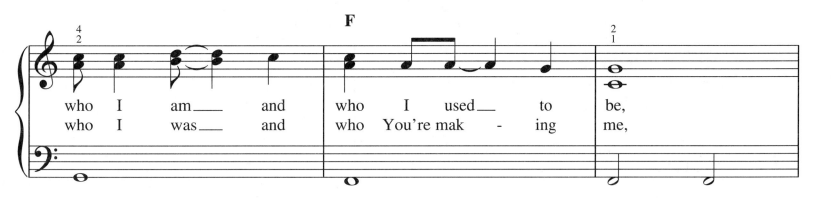

who I am___ and who I used___ to be,
who I was___ and who You're mak - ing me,

some - where in___ the mid - dle you'll find me.___
some - where in___ the mid - dle you'll find

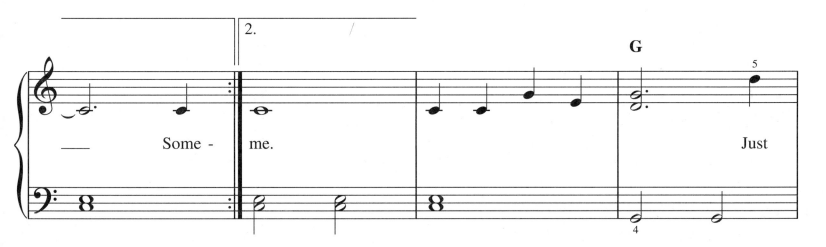

Some - me.
Just

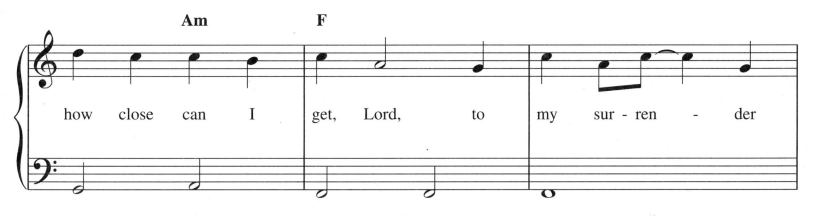

how close can I get, Lord, to my sur - ren - der

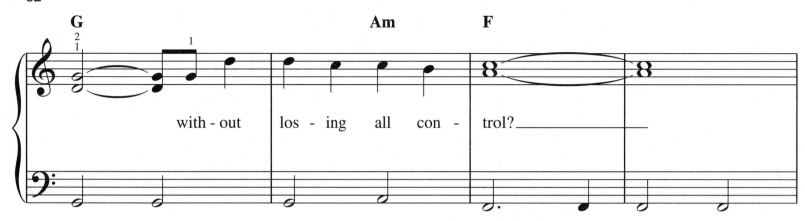

with - out   los - ing   all   con - trol? _____

mf   Fear - less   war - riors in a pick - et   fence,   reck - less a -

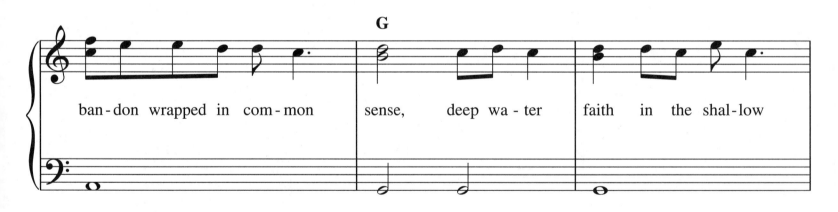

ban - don wrapped in com - mon   sense,   deep wa - ter   faith in the shal - low

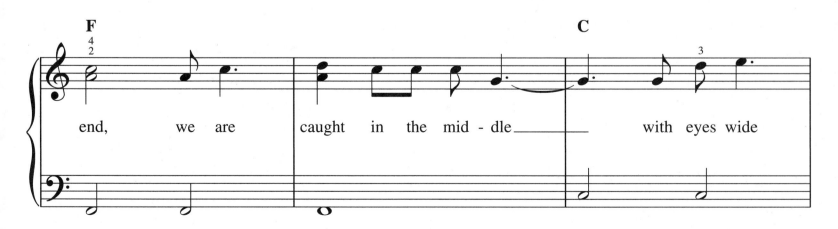

end,   we are   caught in the mid - dle _____   with eyes wide

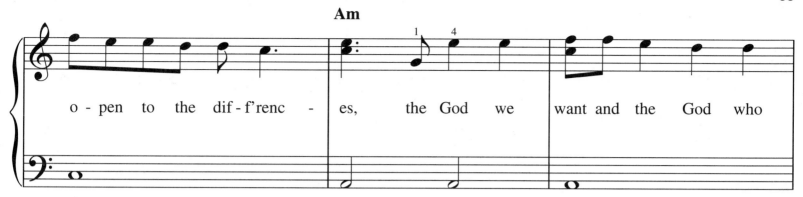

o - pen to the dif - f'renc - es, the God we want and the God who

is. But will we trade our dreams_ for His, or are we

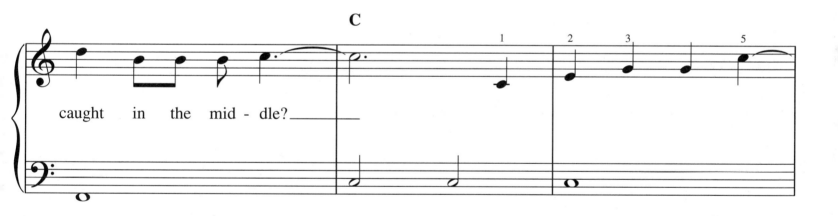

caught in the mid - dle?_____

Are we caught in the mid - dle?_____

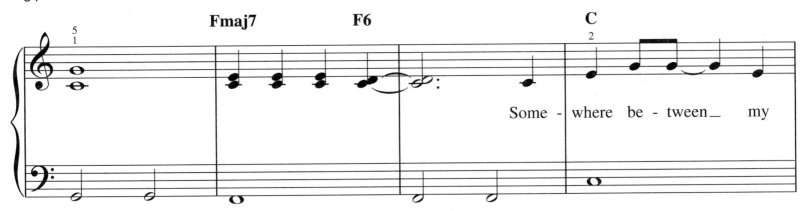

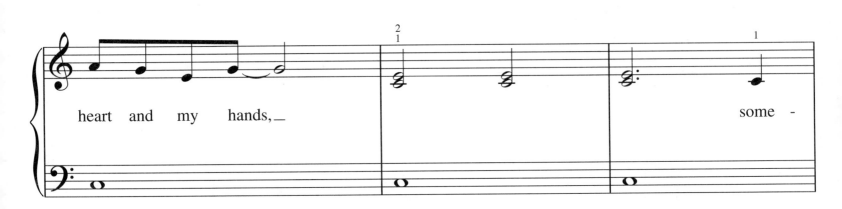

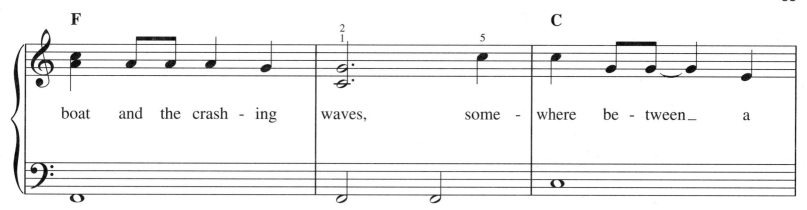

boat and the crash - ing waves, some - where be - tween_ a

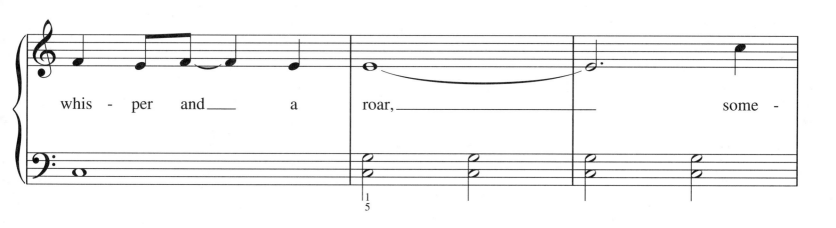

whis - per and_ a roar,_____ some -

where be - tween_ the al - tar and_ the door,_____

_ some - where be - tween_ con - tent - ed peace and

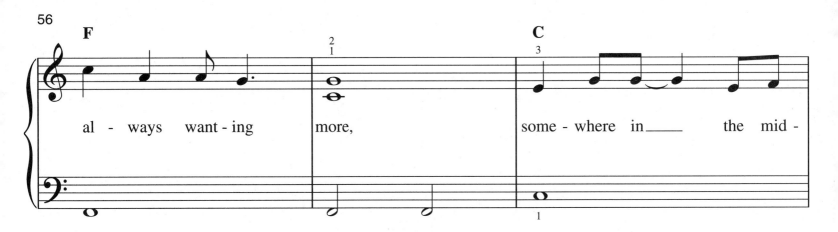

al - ways want - ing more, some - where in ___ the mid -

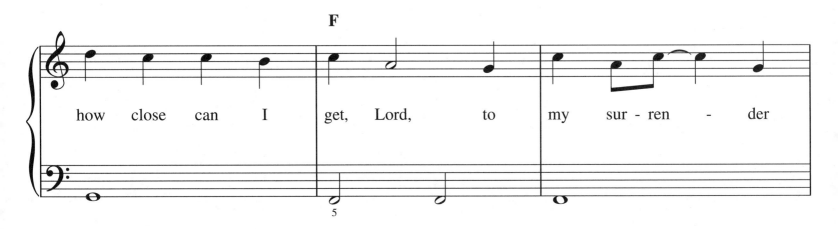

dle You'll find me. ___ Just

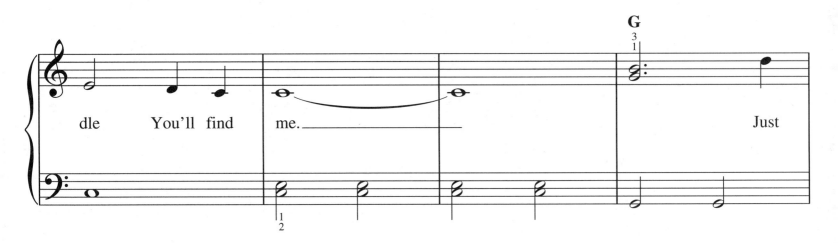

how close can I get, Lord, to my sur - ren - der

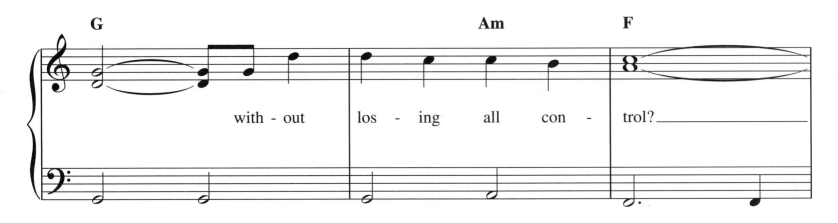

with - out los - ing all con - trol? ___

Fear - less war - riors in a pick - et

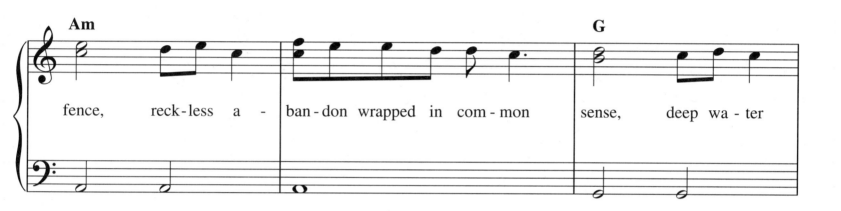

fence, reck-less a - ban-don wrapped in com - mon sense, deep wa - ter

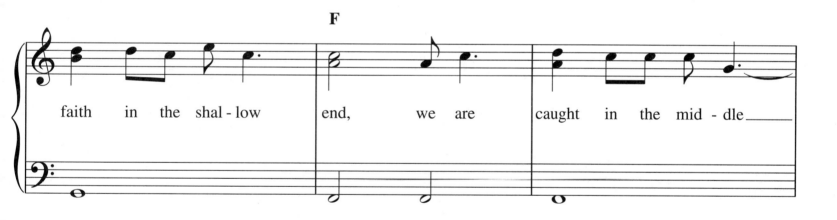

faith in the shal - low end, we are caught in the mid - dle

with eyes wide o - pen to the dif - f'renc - es, the God we

G

want and the God who is. But will we trade our dreams for

F

1.

2.

His, or are we caught in the mid-dle? caught in the mid-dle?

G

F

Lord, I feel You in _____ this place, and I

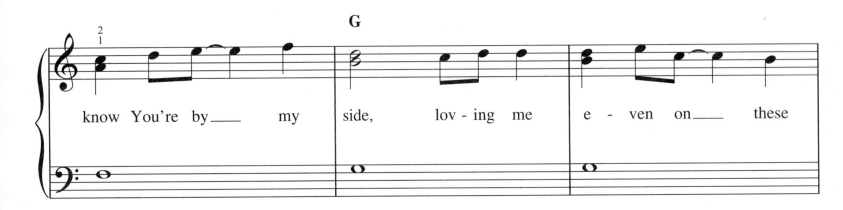

G

know You're by _____ my side, lov-ing me e-ven on _____ these

nights_____ when I'm caught in the mid - dle.

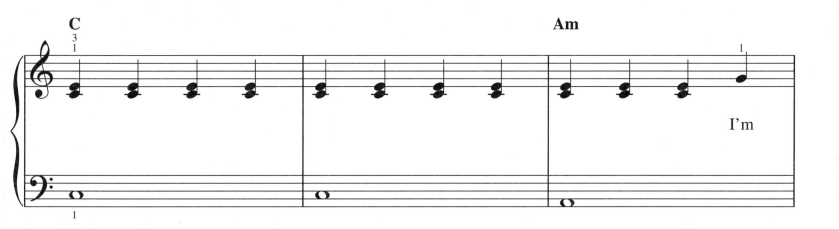

I'm

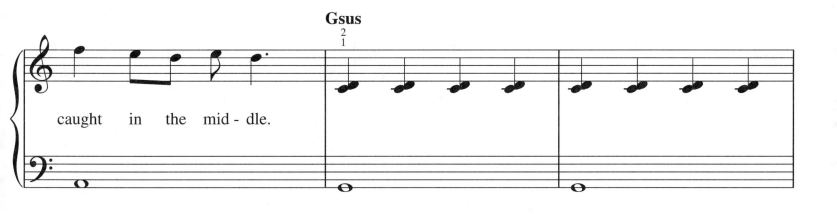

caught in the mid - dle.

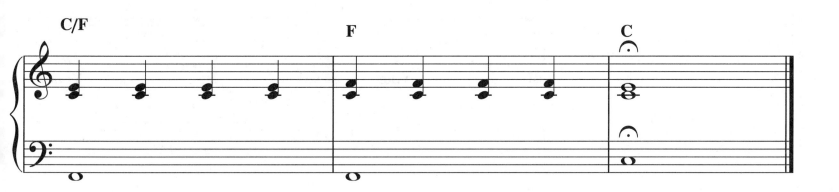

I KNOW YOU'RE THERE

Words and Music by JEFF CHANDLER,
JOEL CHANDLER, JONATHAN CHANDLER,
TIM ELROD and JAMES ROTH

Moderately slow Rock

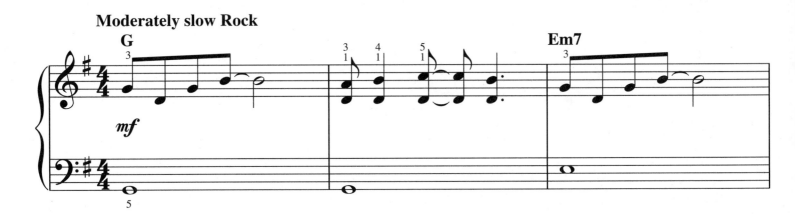

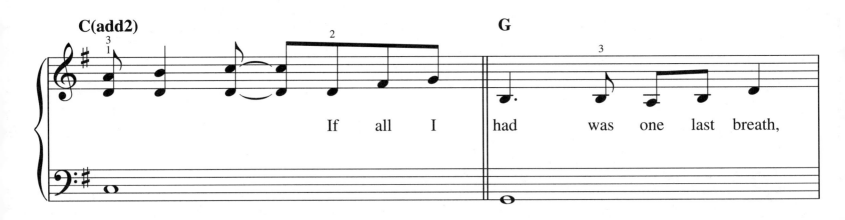

If all I had was one last breath,

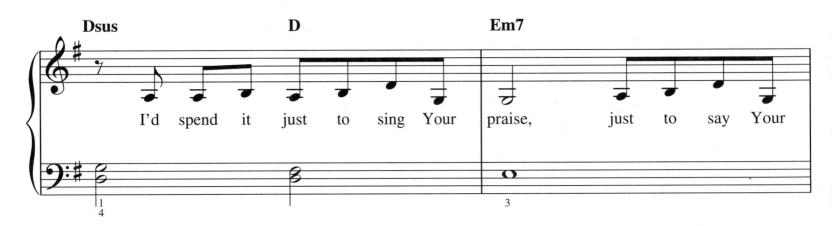

I'd spend it just to sing Your praise, just to say Your

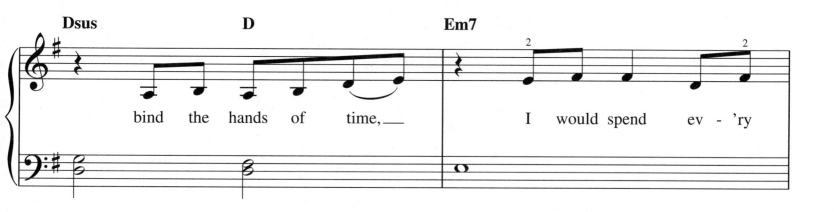

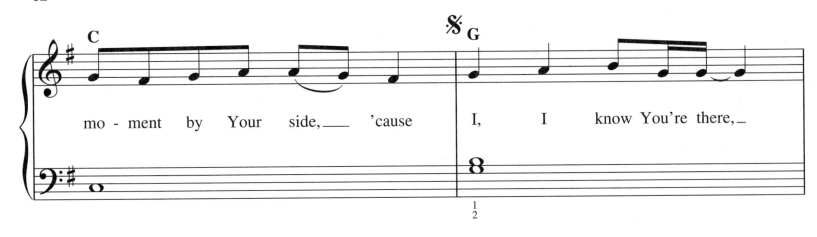

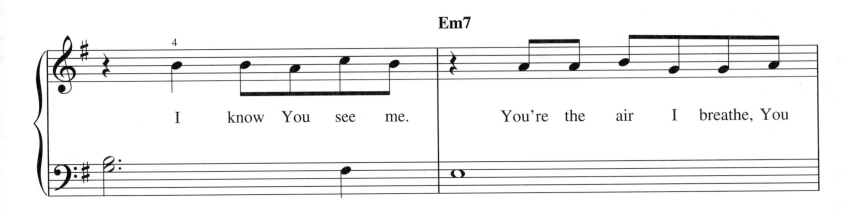

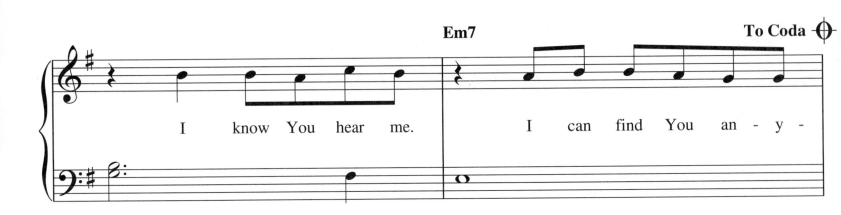

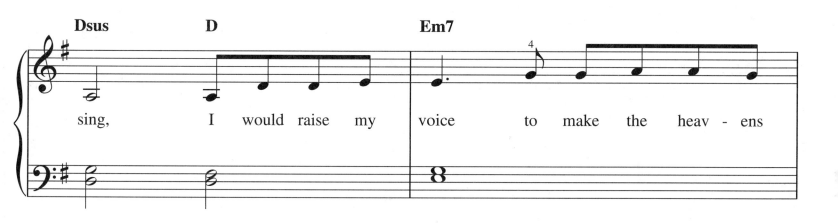

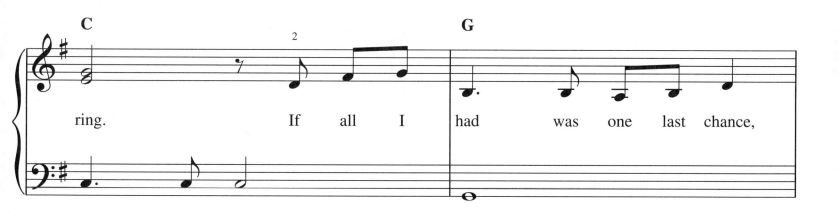

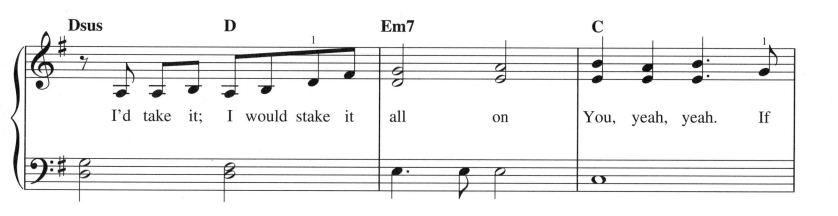

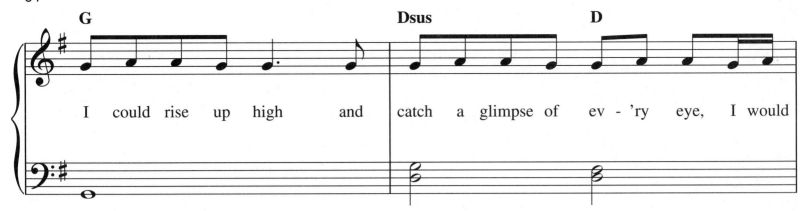

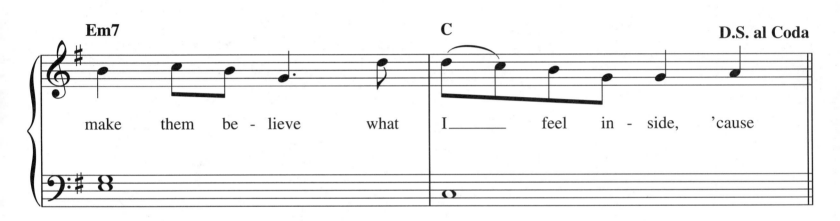

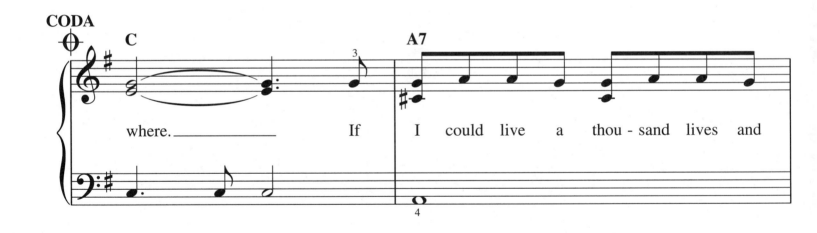

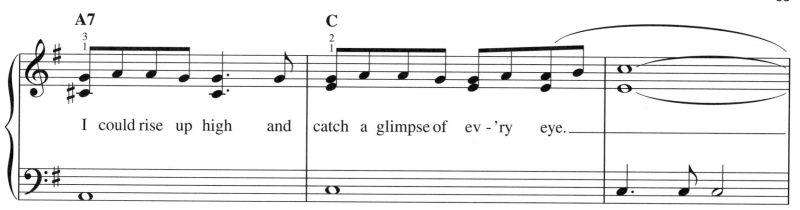

I could rise up high and catch a glimpse of ev - 'ry eye.

I know You're there,— I know You see me.

You're the air I breathe, You are the ground be - neath me.

I know You're there,— I know You hear me.

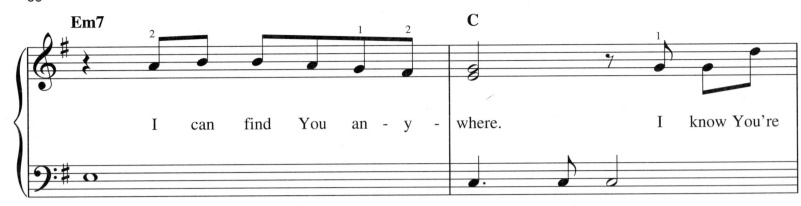

I can find You an - y - where.   I know You're

there, _____   I know You're there, _____

____ I know You're there, _____   You're

there.

PRAYER FOR A FRIEND

Words and Music by
MARK HALL

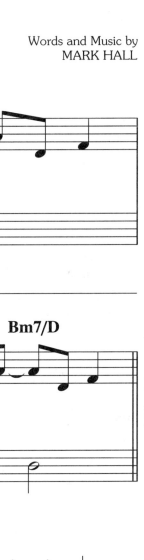

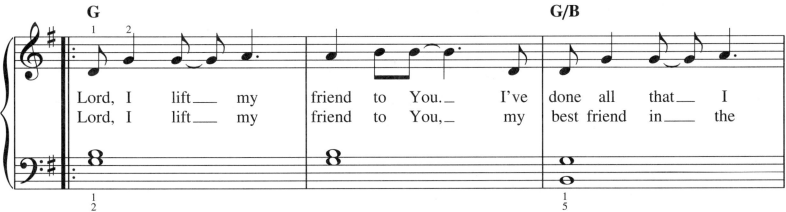

Lord, I lift___ my friend to You.___ I've done all that___ I
Lord, I lift___ my friend to You,___ my best friend in___ the

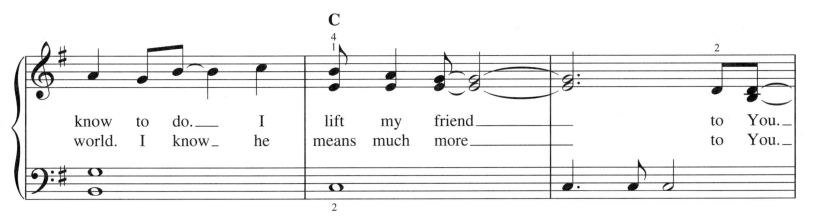

know to do.___ I lift my friend___ to You.___
world. I know___ he means much more___ to You.___

Com - pli - cat - ed
I want so much to

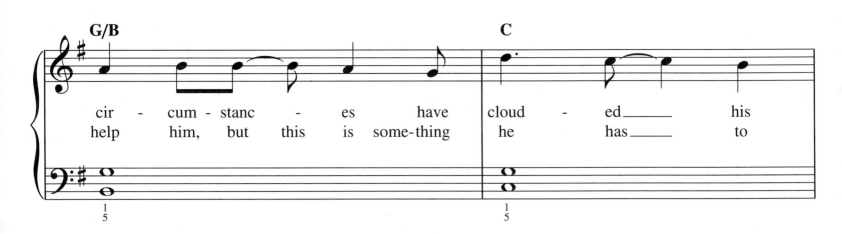

cir - cum - stanc - es have cloud - ed ____ his
help him, but this is some-thing he has ____ to

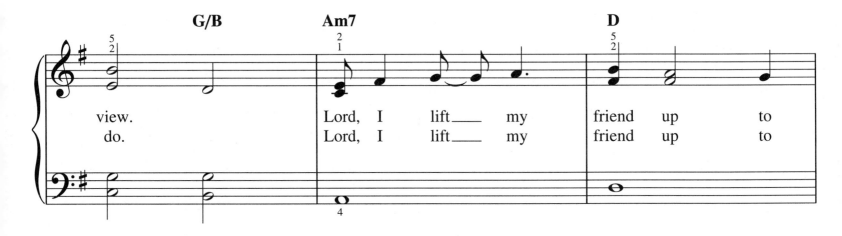

view. Lord, I lift ____ my friend up to
do. Lord, I lift ____ my friend up to

You. I fear that ____ I
You. 'Cause there's a way that ____ seems

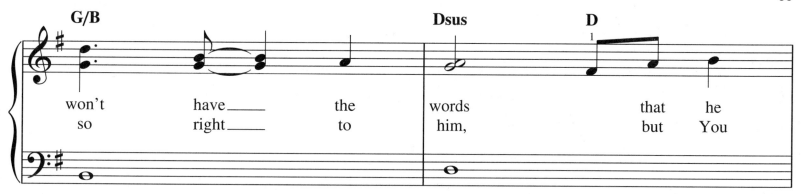

won't have_____ the words that he
so right_____ to him, but You

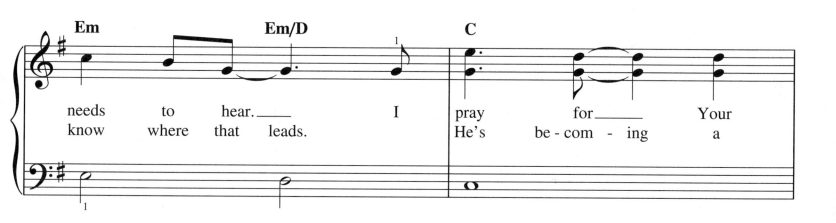

needs to hear._____ I pray for_____ Your
know where that leads. He's be-com-ing a

wis-dom,_ oh God, and a heart that's_ sin-
pup-pet of_____ the world, too blind to see the

cere. }
strings. }   Lord, I lift_____ my

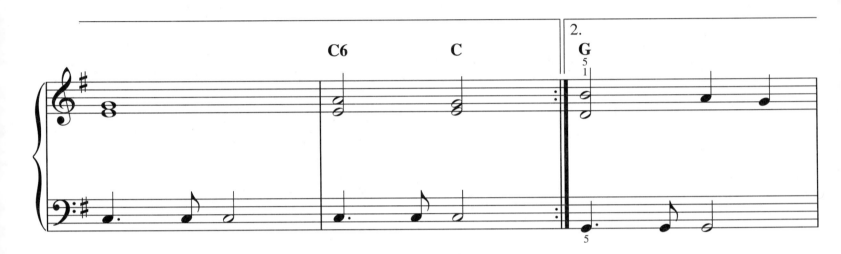

friend   up   to   You.

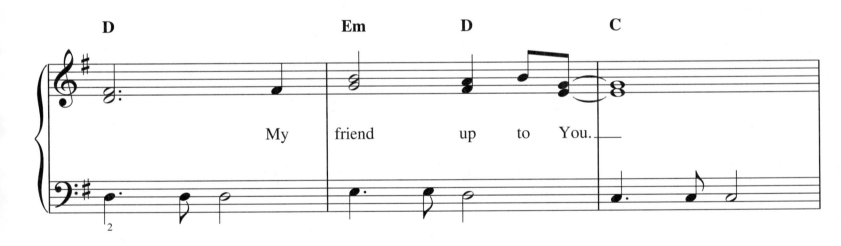

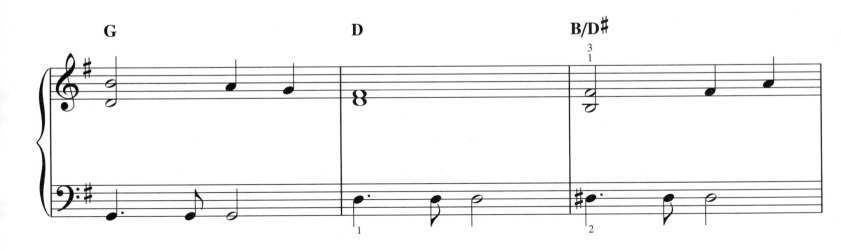

My   friend   up   to   You.

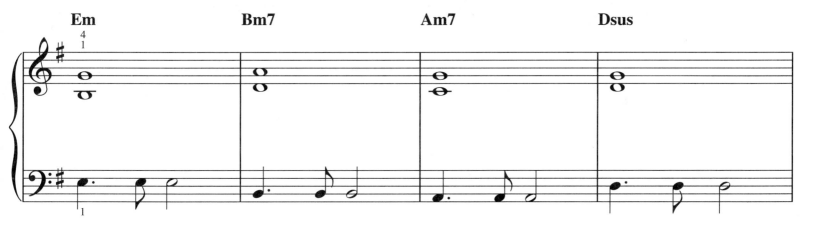

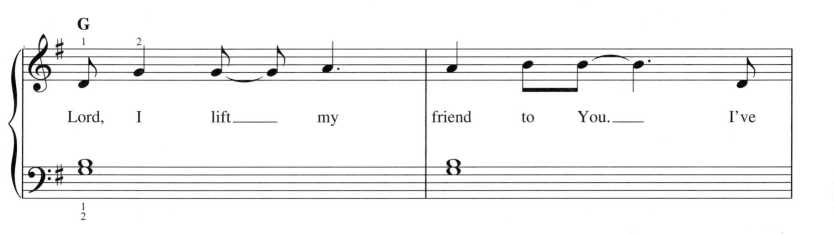

Lord, I lift_____ my friend to You._____ I've

done all that__ I know to do.___ I lift my friend_

to You.__

rit.

ALL BECAUSE OF JESUS

Words and Music by
STEVE FEE

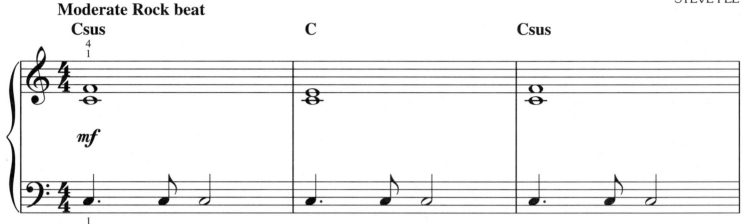

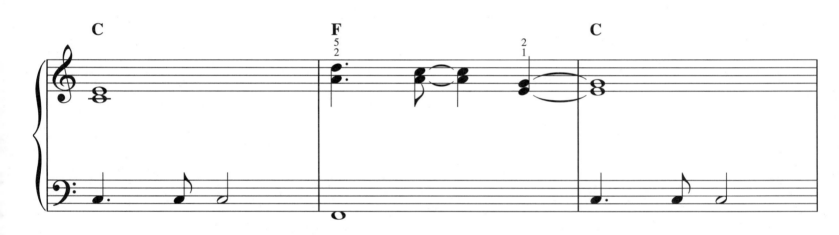

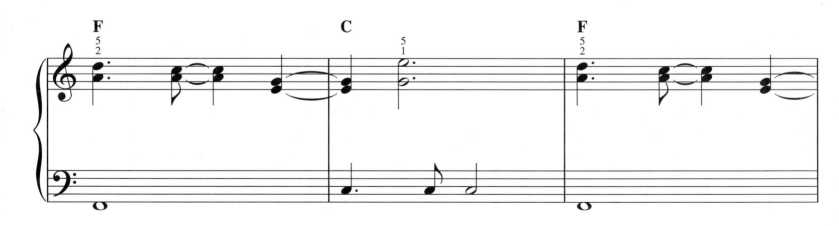

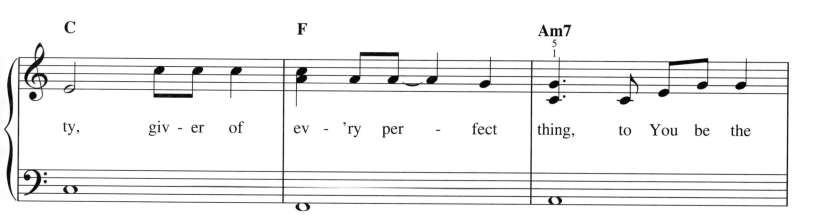

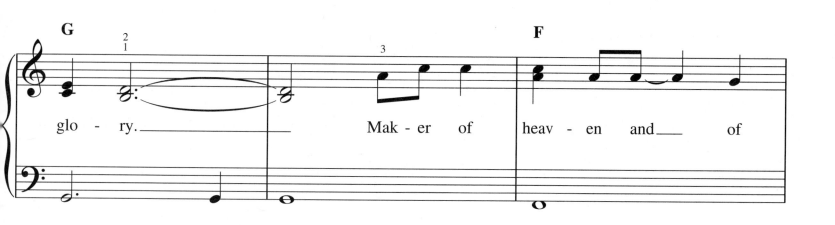

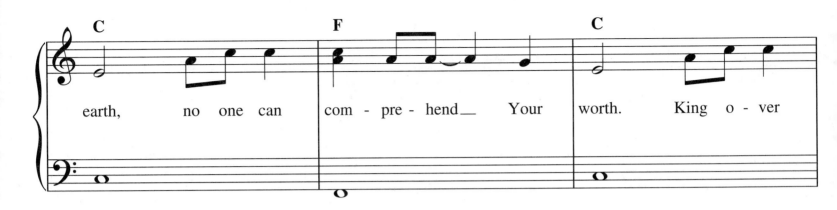

earth, no one can com - pre - hend___ Your worth. King o - ver

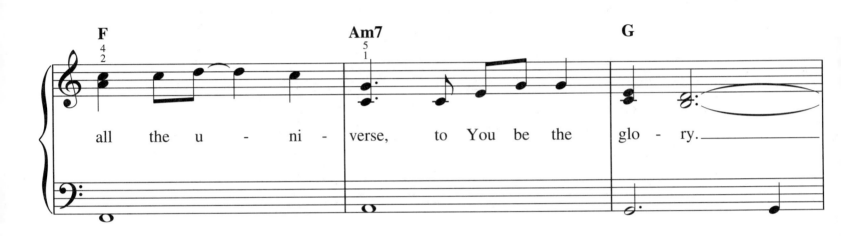

all the u - ni - verse, to You be the glo - ry.___

___ And I am a - live___ be -

cause I'm a - live___ in You.___

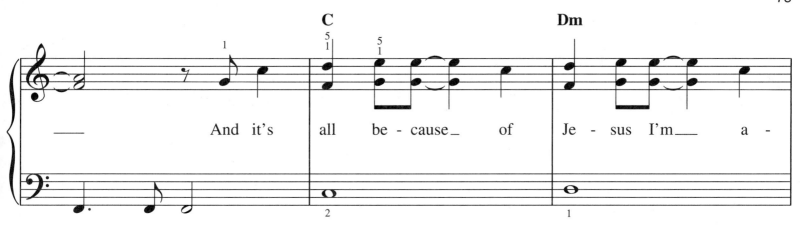

And it's all be-cause_ of Je-sus I'm_ a-

live.___ And it's all be-cause_ the

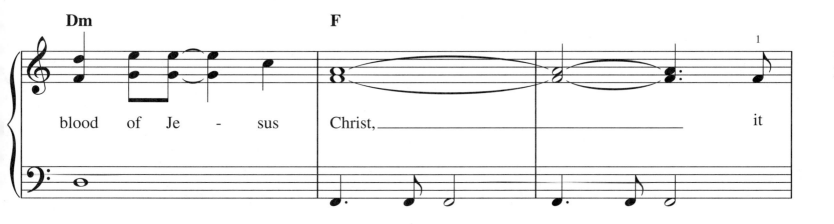

blood of Je - sus Christ,___ it

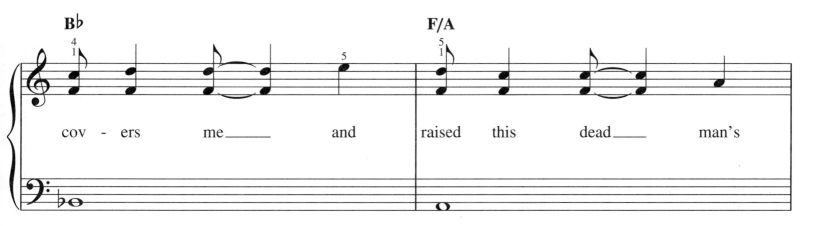

cov - ers me___ and raised this dead___ man's

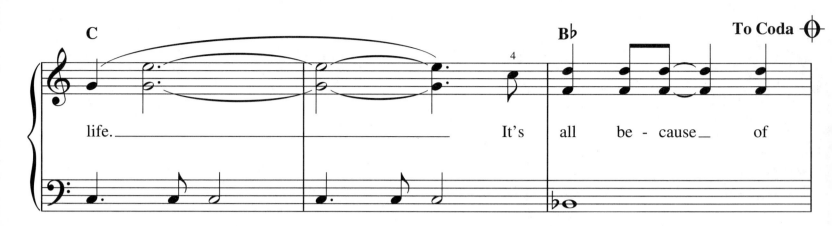

life._____ It's all be-cause_ of

Je - sus I'm a - live.   I'm a-

live,_____   I'm a - live._____

Giv - er of

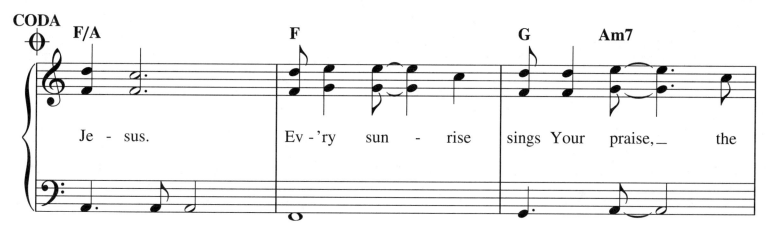

CODA

Je - sus. Ev -'ry sun - rise sings Your praise,___ the

u - ni - verse___ cries out Your praise.___ I'm sing - ing free - dom

all my days,___ now that I'm___ a - live._____

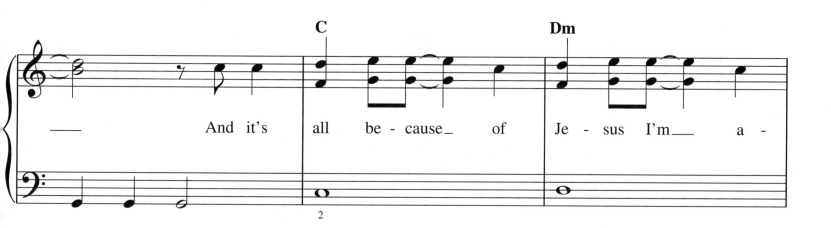

___ And it's all be - cause___ of Je - sus I'm___ a -

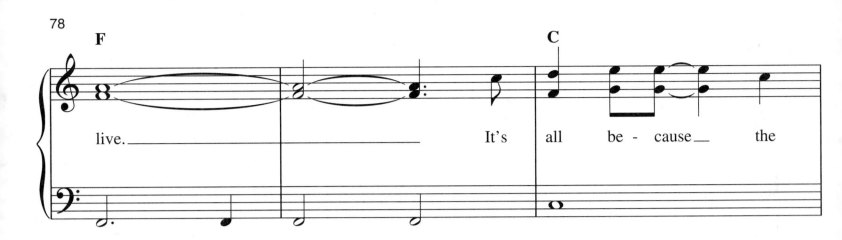

live._____ It's all be - cause___ the

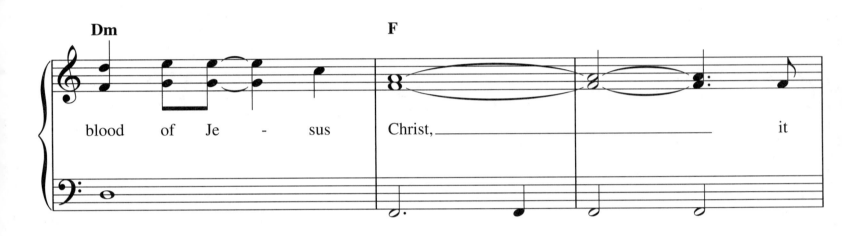

blood of Je - sus Christ,_____ it

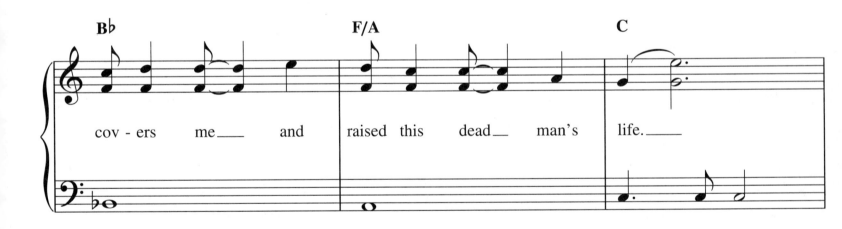

cov - ers me___ and raised this dead__ man's life.___

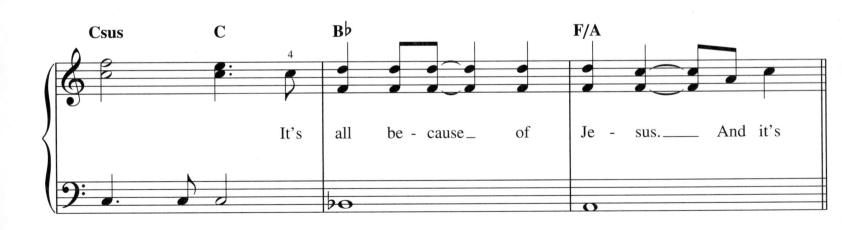

It's all be - cause__ of Je - sus.___ And it's

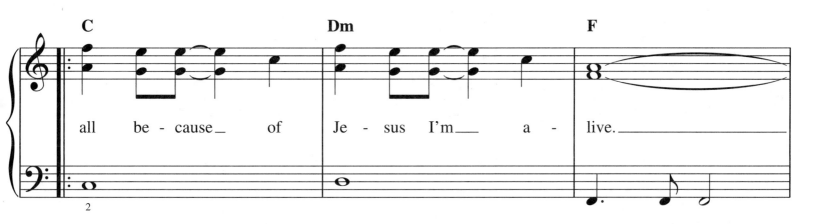

all be-cause_ of Je - sus I'm_ a - live._

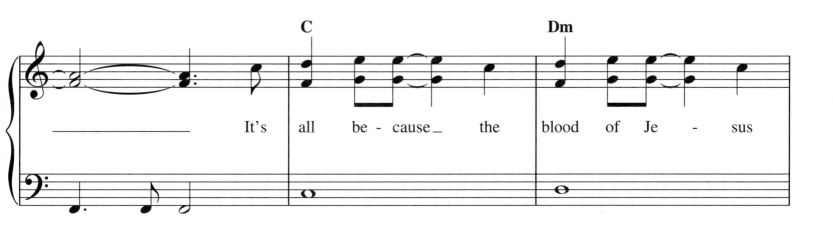

_ It's all be-cause_ the blood of Je - sus

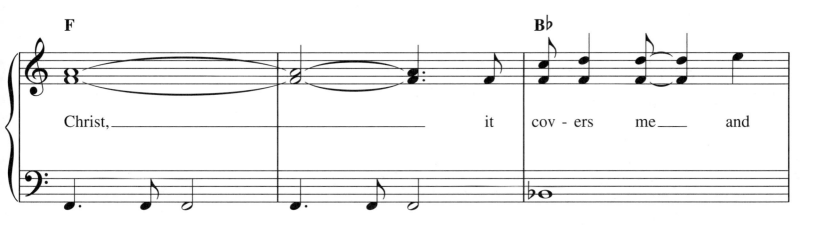

Christ,_ it cov-ers me_ and

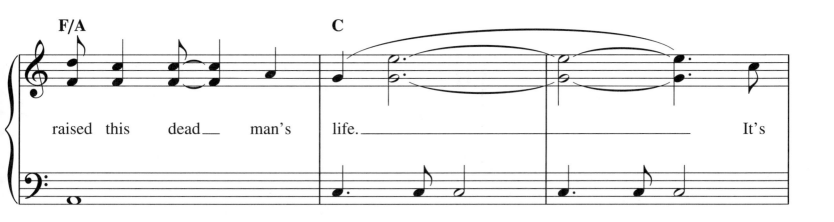

raised this dead_ man's life._ It's

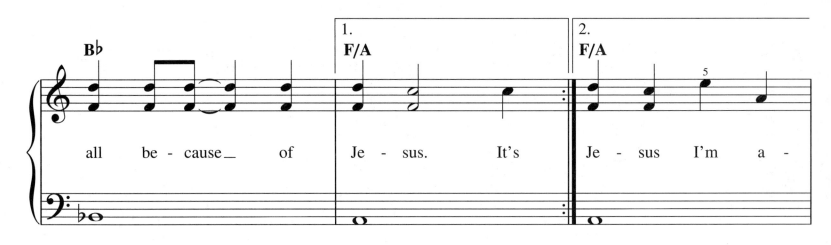

all be - cause— of Je - sus. It's Je - sus I'm a -

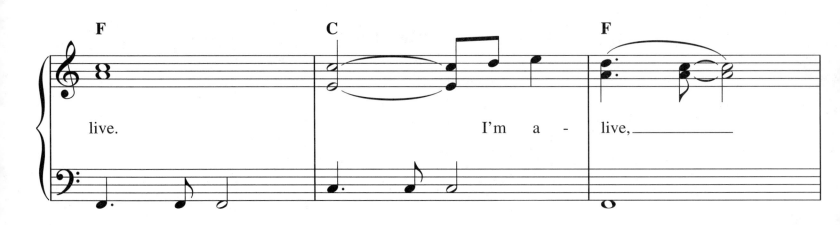

live. I'm a - live,_____

I'm a - live._____

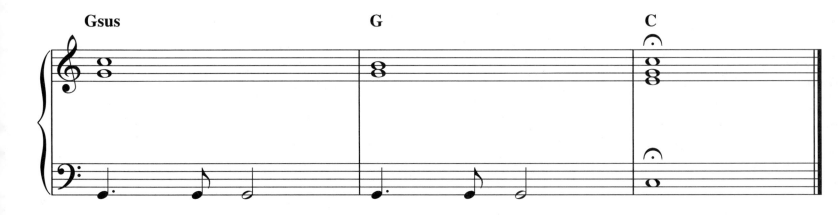